SIDE EFFECTS

THE ART OF
SURVIVING CANCER

CAROLE WEAVER, PhD

Printed and bound in the United States of America
ISBN: 978-0-9980987-0-8

DEDICATION

For Ken

TABLE OF CONTENTS

PROLOGUE

Art has only two purposes—the worship of beauty and the relief of pain.
~ Louise Bourgeois

On May 4, 2007, I was diagnosed with breast cancer after a routine mammography in New Rochelle, New York.

That morning I was in a bad mood as I swung into my little office. My idea for a fund-raiser in the city had been nixed by my boss, the first news of the morning from my assistant, Mynetta. I was miffed.

"It was a great idea: a rich guy gets to sing Frank Sinatra songs at the tony National Arts Club. And it costs the college almost nothing because of my boyfriend's membership," I said.

Mynetta agreed. "And the students would have loved it: karaoke and free eats."

"Maybe a nice gift would follow once he sang, met the students, and then toured the campus on 29th Street," I said.

"Yeah," said Mynetta wistfully. "Shit. Another good idea bites the dust."

My full skirt was long, and the hem caught on the rolling chair as I plumped down at my desk. I yanked it free as the phone rang. Mynetta picked it up.

"Carole, it's Dr. Z."[1]

"Z?" I said.

Dr. Z had been my primary care physician since I worked at Sound Shore Hospital ten years earlier. She was Pakistani, a passionate caregiver, and almost my girlfriend.

"Hey, Z. What's up?"

"Carole, I got your results from the mammography you did yesterday. Um, dear. This is very serious. They're reporting a tumor … it looks malignant."

Her voice was shaking but intent, and I had the sensation that the rolling chair was falling into the floor, except that my skirt kept getting caught in the wheels.

"Oh my God… Z. Maybe the results are wrong. What… uhh…"

My face felt hot. No, I couldn't feel my face. Breast cancer! I was a healthy 63. I take vitamins. I exercise. A crazy commentary unrolled in my head. *I had suffered enough,* my soul screamed. I had a violent mother, the worst pimples of anyone in my teenage world—they were tumors, not pimples—then, really lousy boyfriends, the unexpected death of my father without his seeing his grandchildren and any of my accomplishments; my husband walking out on me with two babies in tow. This job where my ideas were unappreciated. How could I get breast cancer too? How…?

Z's accented voice brought me back to the present.

"I'm going to schedule a biopsy right away. Wait by the phone until I call you with the appointment. It's at the same place you had the mammography."

---

[1] I am using random abbreviations for the names of most of the physicians in this book. At my attorney's direction, this method protects the innocent and avoids identification, a necessary technique because of a legal action which took place later against two of the physicians in the narrative. My general attitude toward the health professionals in this memoir is acceptance of their mistakes as well as gratitude for their part in the miracles which saved my life.

"But at the lab, in the fall, the receptionist looked at my chart and told me that I didn't *need* a mammography. I waited, what, seven months because they told me to wait! And now, cancer? What the hell?"

"We'll discuss it later. Sometimes these things grow quickly," said Z, and hung up.

I had no idea at that point: Z was doing the impossible. Usually you wait a week to get a biopsy. She pushed it through in hours. *Amazing!* I thought, through my fog of self-absorption.

After the biopsy, I spent hours in Z's office staring numbly at her white coat and olive complexion, listening to her slight Pakistani lilt as she advised me and tried to cheer me.

"My friend, Marge, had a double mastectomy—not that you will have a mastectomy—and she's had several lovers since then. She'll know a good breast surgeon. Then there's my friend, Rajmah—he's close in town and such a good doctor…"

Z had known me so long, through my love affairs, bouts of bronchitis, and menopausal hot flashes. In my regular visits to her office, after her medical attention, we talked about our jewelry, the Indian fashion site, utsavfashion.com, and gossip from the hospital. She knew what I needed to hear, especially now: a story about a brave sexy woman with both breasts gone.

But today I was hearing only about one-third of what she said, instead thinking over and over about the tiny tumor probably throbbing inside my right breast. The initial technician was "90 percent sure it was malignant." I shivered at the word. Malignant. It might have been even tinier in October, eight months earlier, when I appeared for the yearly mammogram. I could have caught it earlier … maybe now it is too late. Would it be a simple lumpectomy? Or worse?

I felt virtually naked when I left Z on that Friday afternoon. The special intimacy I shared with my primary care doctor was such a blessing. It somewhat shielded me from what was ahead, I thought, giving me a soft garment around my vulnerability. My family was far away on the West Coast. Telling them could wait until I knew more. But Ken, Ken. I must not only tell him, but also offer him a way out of the journey ahead of me.

But Ken was in Europe, and I would not tell him over the phone. I would have to find other distractions that Saturday and Sunday. I allowed myself a few hours of investigation—an orgy of Internet sites about breast cancer and its various treatments, a terrible idea that only brought me to tears and confusion. A better notion was a stroll with a friend through the White Plains Mall. Apart from Victoria's Secret's brassiere display, the store windows distracted me with summer colors and the thought of a trip to the Delaware beach to see my friend, Mary. *Would I still be able to go?* I wondered. *Was there life after a breast cancer diagnosis?* The unanswered questions tormented me worse than a clear-cut agenda, even one with pictures of surgical knives and poisons dripping into my veins.

When I went back into the college office two days later, everything was the same; and yet everything was different. When Mynetta greeted me, with a tremulous grin, I handed her a bag. Occasionally I had given her clothes she admired, out of girlish affection. This time, I hoped the gift had a meaning she would miss. Inside was the "phone call" skirt, the recalcitrant garment that rolled under the wheels of the chair while I first heard the word "cancer" applied to myself. But she held up the skirt and twirled around with the green fabric held to her waist, with obvious pleasure.

Life before the skirt, life after the skirt—my history in twain.

The medical arc of the following year comprises the major events of this book, an arc which has been marked on the bodies of thousands of women: biopsies, debridements, surgeries, chemotherapies, mastectomies, tattoos, and reconstructions. I salute every scarred darling as I begin. I salute you! Not all have had my remarkable denouement: what began in terror and anguish ended at the sunlit portal of a new life. Although more than 80 percent of women diagnosed with breast cancer survive for ten years or more, the other approximately 20 percent live on in the minds of the luckier ones.[2]

I salute Connie with the compression sleeve who gave me the weak smile across from my chemo lounger; this was her third time. Her chair was empty when I returned two weeks later. My favorite nurse pursed her lips and made the most minimal shake of her head to my question about where Connie was. Metastasis, the stage four engine of death (or just not being able to withstand the onslaughts of well-meaning cures)—these are the finishers of the 20 percent and the nightmares of the 80 percent—the Damoclean swords above our heads for the rest of our lives.

Iconic, the hurt breast conjures sympathy, regret, solicitude, a panoply of sorrows for the loss of beauty, nurturance, and motherly care. No wonder surviving breast cancer is a cottage industry. Our culture acknowledges in books, films, and TV shows the scars and mutilations, the fears of forever carrying the sleeping demon within, the lasting side effects. Even Congress has recognized the effort required to get through breast cancer, with a 1998 law requiring many group insurance plans to cover the cost of reconstruction after mastectomy.[3]

---

[2] American Cancer Society, Cancer Treatment & Survivorship Facts and Figures 2014–2015, http://www.cancer.org/acs/groups/content/@research/documents/document/acspc-042801.pdf.

[3] The Women's Health and Cancer Rights Act (WHCRA), signed into law on October 21, 1998, is a federal law overseen by the U.S. Departments of Labor and Health and Human Services, which helps protect many women with breast cancer who choose to have their breasts rebuilt after mastectomy by requiring many group insurance plans to cover the costs of reconstruction.

Yet, everyone has her (or his) way of navigating the crazy rapids of surviving. Mine involved—as with so many others—friends, more friends, skilled doctors, modern medicine, a little luck, and/or God's grace. But, in my case, some specific objects of art also proved curative. Each piece captured my attention, temporarily eased the physical burden of side effects, offered hints of redemption, and moved me along the path, a path that seemed like the road to Golgotha. As for the art, it was like meeting that one really nice guy who picked up the cross for a couple of minutes—an unforgettable, if achingly brief, relief.

But those few minutes created for me a different world, where the randomness of disease and the fragmentation of life was ordered by somebody else's imagination, someone else's discipline, knowledge, and attention. Art reproached my self-pity and made my soul stand up for its creators. Later in the dark days of treatment, when I felt myself in the midst of tragedy, it struck me that the beauty which artists make is a kind of salvation. After all, great art often grows out of tragedy, springing up from the brutality and hatred in the world. Think of Picasso's *Guernica*, or Boris Pasternak's *Doctor Zhivago*.

Each of these art objects became my personal easement when discomfort and sadness grew too much to bear. Few people knew of my meditations on their beauty, their oddness and intricacies. I preferred to be alone when I looked at them, in a museum where nobody was straining to see over my shoulder. Like a small child's favorite blanket in distress, each one cast a spell with a different magic that calmed my sobs, slowed my breathing, and drained the darkness. Here was the perfect collusion of art's purposes: the worship of beauty was the relief of—at least psychic—pain.

CHAPTER ONE
GUANYIN

The first of these salvation pieces was the Guanyin.

It was the week after the diagnosis, when I was seeing Dr. Z as frequently as her assistant could sneak me in. We were setting up shopping dates for breast surgeons. My boyfriend, Ken, had a beautiful house in the country, and I loved going there. He was an art appraiser, and his home was filled with paintings, sculpture, and most of all, books. It was alive with beautiful, intriguing, exotic things to savor. I needed diversion, another taste in my mouth to wash away the sour palate, worry.

When I left my tiny co-op in Mount Vernon to be with him for the weekend, I told him that I would understand if we broke up—at least for a while—during the treatment for cancer. He brushed off the suggestion. Nothing except my anxiety had really happened yet, but I knew Ken had a deep-seated aversion to hospitals. We had been dating for two years, and I loved him. Yet I was wary of his noncommitment, his cool brilliance. There were too many trips abroad without much explanation, too many days without a phone call, his cool reserve to my heated candor. Stinging lashes were my girlfriends' sideways glances of disapproval when they were around Ken and me. They gave voice to these in their later remarks to me over the phone, like, *"Where is the cherishing?"*

Yet with the health threat looming, I was more determined than ever to enjoy whatever time together we had. I especially loved being

Guanyin, late Chinese

in Ken's home, and it was hard to think of giving it up. It was here where I discovered the artful pieces that tell my story.

In Ken's living room there is a credenza before a window that faces out on acres of wetlands. Several statues of Tibetan gods are displayed here, backlit by moonlight or sun or snow threading through a forest primeval beyond. I relish seeing the gods dancing when I walk into the room, their bronze arms, legs, and faces lifted to silent music or joy. But my eyes always move away to what I call "the queen" of the assemblage, the white porcelain statue that stands just over twelve inches high on a red lacquered stool in front of the dancing gods.

My Guanyin is the Chinese version of an ancient Tibetan god, *Bodhisattva*, who chose not to go to Nirvana but to stay here to help mankind. Like Jesus, this is a Buddha of compassion, one that the Chinese especially love to portray in their own version. The Tibetans called him *Avalokitesvara,* "the Lord who sees everything." But the Chinese wanted the god to be "the one who *hears* everything."

This is my Guanyin, the exquisite god of mercy whose omnipotent ears can hear even the ravishing coos of the infant trying to tell you something, or the sigh rising from the dream of the lover sleeping beside you. But those sounds are the god's delight, not the real duty of the Guanyin, who must own the human cries of childbirth, grief, and imprisonment. Guanyin takes in the hiss of the IED on its way to tearing apart flesh, the imperceptible slit of the surgeon's knife, the catch in my brother's throat when I tell him of my impending mastectomy. The Guanyin hears all, and has pity.

"I love her," I say to Ken, stroking the cool ceramic folds of the gown that seem to sway with her stance.

"Him," Ken corrects.

"Oh no! Look at the grace in her hip, the tilt of her head looking at the little attendant, her long thin fingers," I counter.

He says quietly, "The Guanyin is always a man god. Mercy must be powerful. Beautiful, but powerful."

I am wheedling now. "Woman *can* be powerful. Hera, Athena, the Blessed Mother, Olympic discus throwers…"

Ken recites, "In Tibet, woman is wisdom; man is compassion."

Turning to one of the statues—a male god coupling with his lovely consort on his lap—Ken points a laconic finger. "Compassion fucking wisdom is the story of creation in ancient cultures."

"But my captivating Guanyin may be … a transgender god? A he/she necessary blend for the job of the Big Mercies?" I say, without conviction.

"Look, Carole … your Guanyin has no breasts."

"Ohhhh," I say, with fearful understanding, rubbing the smooth, shiny, white and very flat chest, feeling the shock I felt when I first saw, in *LIFE* magazine years ago, the old-fashioned mastectomy without reconstruction.

This *LIFE* magazine image of a woman with no breasts—that would not happen to me. The surgeries would occur at the same time—the hurt breast gone and a new one appearing, made out of another part of me.

But in those early days in May, I did not know this yet. I was running from the thought of losing anything at all. I was still hoping for a mistake in the diagnosis; someone else's tumor would be discovered soon in place of mine, and my body would be just as pure and unmarked as the porcelain Guanyin I held in my hand. Magical thinking.

CHAPTER TWO
DOCTOR N

I n the weeks following the diagnosis, I searched for a surgeon who
would convince me that I would not need a mastectomy, yet would
give me the best prognosis for survival and no recurrence. I wanted too
much. Each doctor of the three I consulted said that only when they
"went in" could they really understand the extent of the malignancy.

The surgeon Dr. Z recommended was certain. This was Dr. R,
who said I must have a mastectomy for sure. He called me when I
was downtown and leaving a meeting on Park Avenue. I couldn't
hear for the street noise, so I dashed into the first place I could find—
the vestibule of St. Thomas on 53rd Street. I remember holding the
phone to my ear and looking at the magnificent altar as Dr. R expressed his strong prognosis: a mastectomy would almost guarantee
"safety," he said earnestly, and I could avoid radiation.

I thanked him and hung up, so ready to run from his reality that
I could hardly stand still. So I walked 20 blocks that day straight
uptown, my throat dry, my heart full of sand. There must be another
way to safety. A second doctor, highly rated by colleagues, wanted
to do a lumpectomy and then insert, next to the wound, a device I
would wear for weeks; this strategy would generate low-grade radiation, finishing off any errant cancer cells lingering after the lumpectomy. The result would be removal of just the tumor and surrounding tissue. A woman at the college where I worked had done this

and found it palatable, but her tumor was smaller and less invasive than mine. My tumor was not, unfortunately, *in situ* (contained), but rather the cancer was beginning to reach out to other cells and ducts around the malignancy. No surgeon would or could know how much it was reaching out until they "went in." Anyway, I didn't like the idea of a tiny time bomb emanating poison near my heart.

In further exhaustive discussions with Dr. Z, I decided to go to someone I had known before the "day of the skirt," a previous colleague at New Rochelle Hospital who had now become the head of the breast cancer center at another hospital. It seemed like a good bet ... even a feminist flourish. Dr. N was attractive, sexy, and outrageous. When I went to her office, she greeted me in a miniskirt with cowboy boots—a saucy accent to her physician's white coat. With red hair and big smile, Dr. N sported an engaging, sympathetic manner to the women in the waiting room. With all this authority and style too, I thought, *Wow. I have finally found my surgeon.* I watched her expressive face as she spoke on the telephone to the radiologist who was looking at the pictures of my breast in the hospital across the street from her office. How different she was from other physicians—lively, a little kinky, a woman surgeon—hear me roar!

"Oh, we can do a lumpectomy on this!"

"Really?" I was so relieved, my eyes stung.

"Yes, honey. I can get this out and leave you with most of your breast intact."

"Most?" I said.

"Well, you will have an indentation, of course. We'll worry about that later."

She picked up the phone and called the receptionist, "Rita, take a look at my schedule for surgery next week. ... How is May 24th?" said Dr. N, turning to me.

"Nothing sooner?" I said.

"Hey, I'm hard to get. That's 'cause I'm the best."

With all my heart, I wanted to believe her.

Before the diagnosis, Ken and I had planned a trip to Los Angeles to see my family in June. I was hopeful that I could have the surgery at the end of May and leave for California a week or two later. What a reward it would be to see my sons, my brother, my sister-in-law, and niece. This was the plan.

Ken drove me to the hospital on the day of the surgery. There was a little confusion with the paperwork, but by the time Dr. N walked in wearing a purple leather skirt and black Jimmy Choo spikes, all was straightened out. Ken's eyebrows lifted at her outfit, but he said nothing. I kissed him goodbye and let the gurney wheel me into the operating room. A garden-variety lumpectomy. Piece of cake.

In the recovery room, Dr. N's eyes twinkled above her surgical mask. "All went well, Carole."

"Come see me next week."

And she was gone.

Leaving the hospital with Ken felt odd. I seemed rather unfinished, as if the part of me removed, the cancerous lump, was really the me left behind. But to have the lumpectomy "over," this fact I hugged to me, like a teddy bear. This signaled the rest of my life, a happy ending after a misadventure.

I still wanted to have the Memorial Day party at Ken's, a few days after the procedure. We had planned this gathering months before, and I didn't want to lose the chance to show off Ken's house to my friends. To cancel would put, not the happy ending, but the medical episode front and center.

In the soft evening of the barbecue, I relished the big lawn being stroked by a beautiful summer night, the crackling barbecue, and Ken's laughter as he entertained. Gladdened but quiet, I felt surprisingly weak. The entire right breast, not just the surgical site, felt sore, hot, and somehow full, as if I were about to lactate. At one point, I had to sit down to gather my strength. My girlfriends chided me for socializing too soon. "Minor surgery," I reminded them. I just needed a few more days of recuperation. More importantly, we were going to California to introduce Ken to the boys! I had to be well to get on that plane. A little embarrassed, everyone left a tad early in response to my sudden weariness. Sleep was what I needed, I said, as I put my good arm around Ken and pulled him inside the house.

CHAPTER THREE
TROUBLE

The postoperative appointment with Dr. N was brief and troubled. I was happy Ken was invited into the room. After the surgery, while I was in recovery, Dr. N had spoken with him about his attending her alma mater in the '70s, the University of Pennsylvania Medical School. She was impressed that he had studied at such a prestigious school, even though he had never practiced.

Four days after the surgery, Ken and I were in the small examination room with Dr. N. He stepped away from the examination table, giving her room to move around me. I noted this gesture of deference to Dr. N, as she explored the surgical site. The wound near the nipple was red and raw, and there was some black skin, an ugly flap next to the incision; but I thought it was part of the bloody bandage. Ken called it necrosis. As she started to change the dressing, I winced.

Dr. N said, "Well, Carole, be glad. There was no sign of cancer in the lymph nodes, and we got the entire tumor and a good bit of the surrounding tissue. Clean margins. You're good!"

I mustered a smile and looked at Ken.

But he was looking at the physician. Gently, he said, "What about the necrotic tissue? Is that … to be expected?"

Dr. N threw the old dressing into the trash and said, "That sometimes happens. Nothing to be worried about. It will just fall off in a few days."

I tentatively said, "Well, it does hurt a little."

"Sure," said Dr. N, glancing at the wound. "Nothing out of the ordinary. Do you need more Percocet?"

"No. I have plenty of pain pills left. And it's not that bad. Just really sore."

Dr. N replied, "It will be, for a week or so." She finished the bandaging and smiled.

I cut to the chase. "I can still go to California to see my boys and my brother in a few days, right?"

She would have needed a heart of stone to say no to my face.

"Fine! Go to California and enjoy!"

I almost skipped out of the office, but I was careful not to bump my right breast against anything, including my upper arm.

There was just one more hurdle: seeing the oncologist, Dr. T.

Dr. T was a big, handsome man, his large form softened like an ex-football player's. In his 50s, he was a dynamic, white-haired charmer. Trained at Sloan Kettering, Dr. T had an impeccable reputation, and there was no question I had been lucky to get him.

The oncologist is really the quarterback of cancer care, a specialist who coordinates with other physicians, decides on tests, oversees chemotherapy, radiation, and all medications. Most of all, the oncologist is the analyst of your distinct health profile, and the manager of your chances of survival.

There had been some question about whether Dr. T would have room for me among his impressive caseload of patients. But when I talked to his wife, his office manager, on the phone, his association with my breast surgeon, Dr. N, seemed to tip the scales in my favor. I was accepted, and eager to meet him. Until I saw his waiting room that first day.

Every seat was taken, and one person had to stand until a nurse appeared at the door and called a name. When the owner of the name disappeared with the nurse into another part of the office, the person standing could sit in the available seat. Thirty women and some men appeared to be in a club with a dark secret and an unspoken pledge: keep your demeanor pleasant, conversation minimal. In this society, we don't want to know whether you are dying or getting better. Let's not fill the air with how you *really* feel. Let's pretend we are engrossed in the article about the barely familiar celebrity who's been selected for *Dancing with the Stars*. There weren't enough magazines to go around either, so some interchange came from sharing a *Vogue* or *People* once your name was called. Relinquishing the article you were reading to the person next to you, you stood up and faced the music: the chemo room.

All I saw then were the nurses and patients coming in and out. It would be weeks before I went into this *sanctum sanctorum*. Today I just needed to convince my quarterback that I was healthy enough to get into the game. I felt like a kid facing the star player after fumbling the ball. *"Give me another chance, Captain" I said.* I put on more lip gloss and squared my shoulders.

"Caaa-role," sang out the nurse at the door.

In the examining room, after some brief small talk about the operation, Dr. T gently removed the bandage and frowned at the wound. For a big man, he had a much gentler touch than my own surgeon.

His expression said, *I don't like the look of this.*

I whined in my head, *"Don't put me on the bench, coach!"* "Dr. N says it's okay. Normal redness. She said I could go to California this weekend."

He pursed his lips and finally said, "The pressurized cabin may not be the best environment for a wound that's not healed yet. And it looks like it could be infected."

17

Infection! Yikes, I thought. *One of those face masks wouldn't help,* I thought foolishly, arranging my expression back to innocent enthusiasm.

"Dr. N didn't say anything about an infection. She signed off on the trip. It's only a week. And ... it would do me so much good."

He looked at me with a pained smile, reflecting. I could see that he was weighing my need to see my family against the possibility of complications. I would recall later how he avoided criticizing a colleague.

"I'll let you go on one condition. That you take this antibiotic religiously, starting today, and every day you are away. Then you'll see Dr. N immediately when you get back." He was already writing the script for 500 mg of Cephalexin. Meanwhile, I was joyfully getting dressed and thinking about packing. I ran out of the waiting room and drove straight to CVS for the powerful antibiotic, huge white pills that turned out to be useless against a brand-new demon growing within.

CHAPTER FOUR
CALIFORNIA

I slept deeply on the plane, the discomfort in my breast forgotten for a few hours.

I had not seen my West Coast sons and my brother, Vince, sister-in-law, Teryn, and niece, Kate, for many months, and I was levitating with excitement. We went to Culver City to see the place where my brother Vinnie had been writing a TV show, and we all shared a lavish dinner in his home overlooking the Universal Studios. But after a day and a half, I was exhausted. Ken wanted me to go with him to a gala in downtown Los Angeles for an organization raising money for minorities going to medical school. As a volunteer photographer for his friend, Esther, who led the nonprofit, he worked for free at the event, his annual gift to the mission. But that night I was too tired to get dressed and, uncharacteristically, I begged off going in order to stay on the couch downstairs watching movies with Vinnie and my niece. Dressed in his tuxedo, Ken leaned over me for a goodbye and I thought I saw a flicker of worry cross his face.

That night I didn't sleep well, and woke up feeling miserable. Ken was already awake and turned to me as I opened my eyes. He said, "Let's have a look." By this time, the breast was so swollen, I could not put on a bra without pain, so he could easily note the condition of the wound.

Ken got out of bed and, without ceremony or drama, pointed to me and said we must get to a doctor, a breast doctor, as soon as possible. The charade was over, and I knew I was in trouble.

We spent the day trying to reach first Dr. N, then the patient navigator, the nurse administrator entrusted with the surgical aftercare of the patient. The PN told us that Dr. N was not available. Hours later, I spoke again to the PN, who said it was customary to have some discomfort, advising me to take two aspirin and rest. Ken took the phone and insisted we ask for a referral from Dr. N to a doctor in LA. We waited and waited, until finally at the end of the California day, I realized there would be no referral, and that we were on our own. We had to find a doctor ourselves. I thought about Dr. N's leopard skirt and wished instead for the nuns of my childhood, the lavender smell of their long, black cotton habits, their clean hands caressing my hair. *They* would have called me back with a colleague's number in LA.

Thank God for my sister-in-law, Teryn, who had a close friend working, as it turned out, for the head of breast surgery at the USC Cancer Center. She was the scheduler of his appointments, and managed, with Teryn's imploring pressure, to get me an appointment the next day. Before we drove to that appointment, I called Dr. N one more time, leaving a message with the attendant that I urgently needed to speak to her about another doctor in LA.

Again, no reply.

Dr. H performed an aspiration without anesthesia, draining the infection. There was no time for an elaborate setup, and he warned me ahead of time about the pain. Holding the nurse's hand throughout, I endured the ordeal, made worse by the psychological strain of Dr. N's evasion in not responding to my calls. She was the head of her department in New York just as he was the director of a parallel division in Los Angeles. Yet he was handling *her* negligence. I was furious, but too much in distress to address my embarrassment. Dr. H's face said it all about his impression of my medical care.

When the procedure was over, Dr. H showed me that he had removed a Coke bottle full of fluid from the breast, noting with a disturbingly serious tone that he had never seen such a bad infection. He would have kept me in the hospital, except that I was scheduled to return to New York the next day. Ordering that I be put on an IV with antibiotics at least for a few hours, he sent for a pathology report on the extracted fluid. Finally, this West Coast angel, as I came to see him, inserted a drain in my breast wound, commenting on drains being standard procedure for lumpectomies, an oblique reference to Dr. N's somewhat unorthodox protocol in not providing one.

I was terribly worn out from the pain of the aspiration and the handling, but overwhelmingly grateful for Dr. H's compassion and grace. Now I was eager to get home and get the infection properly addressed by my own doctor. With the fluid released from the wound, the pain was considerably reduced, although I spent the flight home worrying.

A day or so later, I saw Dr. N again, and that appointment nearly convinced me that I needed a new doctor. But who and where? I thought I could at least convince her to consult with Dr. H in Los Angeles. First, when I asked her to make the call, she refused, pulling out the drain with disgust and throwing it into the trashcan. I was so shocked. I did not note until later that she should have had a pathology report on that "trash." But she wanted to do another aspiration. I begged her not to, but she insisted that the fluid had to be released. Again, without anesthesia. This time, the procedure was so painful that I begged her to stop only a minute or two into the process. My friend Joan, who was outside waiting for me, became upset with my screams and asked the nurse if she could help.

The drama of the scene was exhausting me, yet I needed to know the results of the test. I felt I couldn't call Dr. H myself to get the results. Doctor to doctor seemed to be expected for the truth to emerge and protocol to be honored. More than anything, I wanted Dr. N to talk to Dr. H, and I left imploring her to call him. That was the last time I saw Dr. N. Joan and I went to lunch, but I toyed with my soup and finally blurted out my deep worry to my old friend. I needed to see Dr. Z.

The weekend came and went while I turned over my options, and hoped that the report from California would validate Dr. N's treatment. I saw Z on Monday, an appointment which turned my world upside down. It was a tumultuous meeting. Dr. Z looked at the breast and immediately diagnosed gangrene, and advised hospitalization immediately. I was terrified, and asked her to call Dr. H in California. On the phone to him, she requested the results of the pathology report. He told her *E. coli*.

I was in the room when Z's face told me that this was an incredibly serious infection. Z's two assistants ran from the room and told the other waiting patients that the office would be closing. I did not realize the implications of an infectious disease. If the two or three people in the waiting room had open wounds, they might also contract the virus!

For the first time, Z called Dr. N, but I did not hear the conversation. I only heard the tone in Z's voice, and it was harsh and brief. She turned to me and said that I needed attention from a disease control doctor, that I had to get to a hospital soon. At the same time, Z quelled my panic. I could see in her demeanor shock at her colleague's negligence.

CHAPTER FIVE
DECISION

The next day I ran to the shelter of Ken's house to get advice and mull over my options. Should I go back to Dr. N and to the hospital where I might have gotten this deadly disease? Should I go to New Rochelle, which is closer to my home, where I know people from working there six years ago?

Its reputation wasn't great, but the Joint Commission—the regulatory agency which grades hospitals and makes sure standards of care are maintained—was just now going through the institution. There was no better time to put my life in the hands of this hospital in New Rochelle, especially since I knew some of the physicians.

But it would be a bold move. Who had ever heard of firing their breast doctor? Dr. N would expect me to go back to the hospital where she practices, where I got the infection in the first place. To find another doctor at another hospital felt like jumping off a cliff! But when I turned from the chasm below, I saw only a monster.

I needed a place of calm and beauty in order to make an enlightened decision. Ken urged me to come and stay the night, enjoy the garden, and talk about the plans for the Mexican suite to be created upstairs. This might be my last hours of serenity and joy for a while.

When I arrived, Ken was with a client, so I occupied myself with one of my favorite rooms in the house. It was a small den where there was a cabinet he called a *schatzkammer*, a place to keep little precious objects,

Small jade cup, circa 1795

the A-list in a house full of treasures. There was a foot-high vase made of lapis and some Tibetan prayer containers, rather like evening purses made of brass. Some tiny netsukes—the Japanese belt buckles, a few inches square, exquisitely carved of ivory—and small statues of deities.

My favorite thing here was a white jade cup about 8 inches high and 5 inches wide. It was clearly a royal vessel with its carved handles and square base, and I loved to hold it up to the light and marvel at its pale green luminescence. Ken's house was always cool, but the jade chalice felt slightly warm, I imagined, as if a diminutive prince had just held it in contemplation. It retained the warmth of his touch. The proportion of its parts seemed perfect for a tiny emperor, who would sip from the rim with its small symmetrical dragons on each side. The Greeks were right: beauty has much to do with mathematics. The famous statue of David in the Uffizi Gallery may owe its magnificence to its perfect height—seven times the measure of the head was considered to be the ideal human proportion for height. One Roman architect was even fussier about the relative lengths of hands, forearms, chin to hairline, foot, and chest.[4] Michelangelo was obsessed with measuring statues, corpses, and living models. He chose eight heads as the full measure for an ideal statue, Dürer chose seven and a half heads, and Giacometti twelve! How that explains the long skinny Giacometti figures!!!

Perfection of the human form! Even in my young and nubile days, I had never had nearly perfect breasts. They were too small

---

[4]The mathematical study of the human form was a preoccupation in the classical age. The Roman architect Marcus Vitruvius Pollio (31 BC to 14 AD) described the perfect body in *De architectura libri decem:* "... the head from the chin to the hairline measures one-tenth of the entire body. Likewise, the flat or extended hand from the wrist to the tip of the middle finger is equal to the distance from the chin to the part of the hair; i.e., one-eighth part. ... The length of the foot is one-sixth of the body length, the forearm one-quarter, the chest one-quarter."

then; and in my 60s, they were heavier, but hardly perky. I had a scar on my nose from skin cancer, and that nose was too wide anyway. My thighs were always too big, with a texture like cottage cheese, and calves too muscular.

Arms, flabby from waiting on tables and carrying huge trays in my 20s, a workout for years, followed by arms subdued by library desks, long hours of typing, or merely opening books. Except for massive tomes at the Folger Shakespeare Library, books were lighter than a two-foot silver tray with eight filet mignon dinners, lifted as high as I dared above my right shoulder. As I went from waitressing to scholarship, the flaccid years settled in. I had many scars, in fact, on my face and body, from surgical removal of at least a dozen sebaceous cysts throughout the years. After living for six decades, I had braved the skid marks of time. And there were more ahead.

Perhaps this history was what comforts about a perfect form held in the hand, or captured by the eye. A craving for smoothness, balance, symmetry—*ahh*, at last satisfied.

The cup: a dragon for each side and two handles, a metaphor for the decision I must make between going back to Dr. N or going forward into the unknown. I am the cup, the hollow, at the center.

The last time I looked at the cup before I left for the hospital, I thought of Christ in the garden, and his moving request to his father: "Let this cup pass from me."

No chance of that for either of us.

Dr. Z called me twice while I was at Ken's, but she would not advise me either to stay with Dr. N or to find another doctor. Just, she ordered, get to some hospital. Finally, on the morning of June 12, Ken drove me to the emergency room at the hospital in New Rochelle.

My first step was to meet with the epidemiologist who would evaluate my infectious status. I was on a gurney for six hours, waiting for examinations, talking to Dr. Z on the phone, and most of all trying to find a new breast surgeon who would take my case.

Dr. N finally called. This was her first phone call to me. I thought about how I had longed to hear her voice when I was in California. But at this moment, only a few days later, sitting on the emergency room gurney, I didn't want to speak to her. *How do I fire my breast surgeon?* I wondered.

"How are you, Carole?" said Dr. N, cheer covering a slight tremor in her voice.

"I'm not well, Dr. N. I've been diagnosed with *E.coli*. I'm at Sound Shore Hospital and I've decided to be treated here."

"Why don't you come to my hospital in Queens? I'll operate on your breast right away."

I inhaled sharply and blurted out, "I've lost faith in you, Dr. N. Forgive me, but I don't trust you anymore. The necrotic tissue … You ignored it and Dr. H's advice. You threw the drains into the trash. I don't want to go back to the place where I probably got this infection."

Her voice was imploring, even wheedling. I don't remember what she said. Only the sound of that voice.

I mumbled my goodbye and hung up.

Meanwhile, the emergency room physician was exasperated with me. "Either find a doctor or leave," she insisted. I would've called her a bitch, but I needed that gurney!!!! I begged for more time and the chance to be examined by another doctor. Perhaps this doctor would agree to treat the breast, give me the medications I need, and put me back on the path to what? Chemo? Radiation?

Finally Dr. B, the infectious disease doctor, examined me and took a sample for her lab, and then a picture of my breast. I began to breathe more easily.

Dr. B was the antithesis of Dr. N: serious, no makeup, no non-sense. Much later I would discover that Dr. B is also a dedicated amateur opera singer! The doctor who gave me the greatest relief in the ER was an artist in both healing and music. Dr. B's musical art is sustaining, but invisible. On stage, she was colorful and passionate (I found out later); in the emergency room, quiet and focused. Without alarming me, she made it clear that we needed to address the infection with medication immediately. Despite the scare of a disease that sounded like a plague out of Africa, her procedures calmed me. At least, I realized at the time, I am being cared for by a steady hand. I knew also that Dr. Z respected her immensely. I started to feel some sense of control.

Finally, I was receiving proper attention for the infection; but at this point there was still no doctor who would agree to clean up the mess that was now my right breast. Because, I realized, it was the work of another doctor! Surgeons are like cowboys: they want to shoot first, not follow another's gunplay, especially since the wound was now riddled with infection.

No breast doctor was on call at the time I was in the ER, so I reached out to a surgeon I knew of, a relative of one of my students. After I spent several hours waiting, Dr. P hastened into the ER cubicle, dressed in a white shirt and tie, open at the collar. I could see the sweat stains under his arms.

"Hi, Dr. P. Thank you so much for taking the time..."

Interrupting me, he opened the hospital gown and quickly looked at my breast, his face melting into ill-disguised disgust.

"This is infected. I am not used to working on such a botched job."

"But, the surgeon didn't do this! It is because of the *E. coli*! And... do you always talk to patients in this way?"

Despite my anguish, I had to stand up for myself. Even if it meant getting rid of the only surgeon I had seen all day!

"How dare you treat me with disgust!"

He turned and left the room. My one regret is that I didn't TELL him to leave.

At this point, I took matters into my own trembling hands.

At last, even without a surgeon, I decided to be admitted into the hospital under the care of Dr. Z and Dr. B, the infectious disease surgeon. They put me in a pleasant room, which was semi-isolated, which meant no roommate. Immediately the nurses hooked me up to an IV and administered three antibiotics. Dr. B was not taking any chances. She was mobilized to fight *E. coli*.[5]

I was in this semi-isolated state for ten days—although the room felt busy so much of the time with nurses, interns, and doctors, not to speak of friends in and out, that I hardly felt alone. I rather yearned for peace, especially at night; but the monitoring and attention of the nurses was incessant. Apparently, for the medical team, I was somewhat of an oddity, with my ravaged breast and its rare infection contracted in a supposedly sterile operating room. (Later, my attorney surmised that the *E. coli* may have entered the breast during the biopsy in the radiology lab. There is no way of knowing where I came into contact with it. One thing was certain: a wound would have been a likely entry point, whether the tiny hole of a biopsy needle or the more vulnerable opening of a surgical cut.)

The next day, Dr. Z called me with relief in her voice. It was a welcome change. She had found a surgeon who agreed to her pleadings to operate. Obviously a good friend of Dr. Z, he was not a breast

---

[5]*Escherichia coli*, or *E. coli* for short, is a common bacterium. Hundreds of different strains exist, some of which live in intestines. Most are harmless, but certain strains of *E. coli* can cause severe diarrhea and infect the genital and urinary tracts. It can be fatal. Most often, *E. coli* comes from eating raw or undercooked ground beef or drinking raw milk. The bacterium is mostly found in animal feces. Less commonly, it can be transmitted from one person to another, usually by direct physical contact.

surgeon but a vascular specialist who would take care of the wound as soon as he had an opening in his schedule. The identity of this doctor is one of the only two names I want to reveal among all the doctors in these pages. As ever gracious, he agreed to allow me to use his perfect name: Dr. Karanfilian (pronounced *care an feel in*).

When I heard this, I imagined him holding the jade cup and drinking deep.

CHAPTER SIX
STABBY MOMMY

After great pain, a formal feeling comes.
~ Emily Dickinson

Dr. Karanfilian performed the most urgently needed surgery soon after I was admitted, but this was only the beginning of procedures. Along with these came almost constant discomfort.

The pain I endured before chemo was, in a way, the worst physical pain of that year. Surgeries and debridements, especially the one without anesthetic, changed me permanently, not only by giving me additional physical scars. The most dramatic incident was one in the middle of the night: after a particularly long operation, a blood vessel in the breast burst and the night physician and the chief resident came to my bedside, where the sheets were soaked with blood.

"If we move you to the operating room now, you will lose more blood," said the chief resident, who often did the daily dressing. "We think we can cauterize the wound right here to make the bleeding stop."

"Will you work with us, Carole?"

What followed was an intense 20 minutes of the two men trying furiously to isolate the vein and stop the flow of blood. I guess to keep me calm, they did not turn on the overhead light, but used the bedside lamp as a spotlight on the right breast. An intern held a flashlight over their heads. The resident, my favorite Dr. Venn, constantly hushed me.

"If you cry, I can't do this," he insisted in a low tone. "You can't move."

Barely breathing, I felt I had to say something, so it became a whispered, "OK. OK. OK. OK."

So I held out my arms to the probing and sewing by repeating the acceptance. Affirming, affirming.

Astrophysicists say we must always look up at the stars to remember what we are made of. The strangeness of this hospital setting and my incantation of "OK" reversed the vision. Instead, I was looking from a high place *down* on that blood-soaked bed with the two doctors surrounded by darkness, working in a circle of light as they knelt next to me. Cosmic was my perspective, and oddly prophetic: I was among the planets as I watched. This was *Star Wars*, the movie, and I was the Jedi. I had mind tricks for survival.

When it was done, I felt such gratitude and peace, as if I had reached the other side of something once and for all. Was this the "formal feeling" Dickinson writes of, which follows "great pain"? I used to think the poet meant the soul dons a tuxedo for a while. Now I know the formal feeling is a benign distance from the immediate.

When I turned to my familiar prayers and the Catholic images I grew up with, religion let me stand back from the overwhelming detail of the wound in the breast. Misery, said one philosopher, may come from wallowing in something small that is horrible or distasteful.[6]

We forget the larger goodness of our lives. God and the soul are triggers of expansion, rockets to a higher place, so that the tiny dark

---

[6]Mark Nepo, *The Book of Awakening: Having the Life You Want by Being Present to the Life You Have*, originally published in 2000; reissued in 2011 and available in various formats and editions.

thing can be lost. My ugly wound could be swallowed up in a bigger, kinder picture.

And so, I manipulated my mind to manage the pain.

Daily, the residents would come into my room to change the dressing. Like tentative white birds expecting a feast of breadcrumbs, they would file into my room and cheerfully, with obvious strain, greet me. I withstood that pain through imagination, memory, and reminding myself of the television news from the night before. The war in Afghanistan was raging, and the death tolls of the young men would be read each night. In silence, there was the picture and the name of the dead soldier: "Joseph McNally, from Fort Worth, Texas, age 22." When the sweet blonde medical student held my hand, and the chief resident—a brilliant young doctor with a distressingly dirty white coat—handled the wound, I would imagine the mother of the dead 22-year-old and say to myself, "This could be worse."

When I dreamt during those nights in the hospital, I would think about my childhood saints. Schooled by nuns since I was five years old, my very soul is etched with the rich Catholic culture of passion, especially those images of the crucifixion, the agony of martyrs, the torments of hell that make up the Western world's catalogue of great art. Since I was a little girl, the statuary in the churches I frequented, the holy pictures I got for winning handwriting contests, the art books I was taught by; and later, as a young woman, the museums in Europe I wandered through on my way to a romantic assignation; the cathedrals, the squares, the chapels in Italy and, lately and especially, the Mexican churches I had visited with my lover, Ken, all celebrated extravagant pictures of pain. Stephen King had nothing on these horrors.

And, now, hospitalized and quarantined, I conjured in my sleep some of my holy friends. At age eight, I was introduced to—arrows

Madre Dolorosa, the Church of the Holy Cross, Salamanca, Spain

through your gut and everywhere else? Hello, St. Sebastian! Then, at nine, who was that being stretched on a wheel? St. Katherine, of course. Upside down on a cross so the blood rushes to your brain and eventually makes it explode? St. Peter, the so-called Rock of the original church. Then there was Lucy, who was blinded, and somebody else who ate the pus of terrible sores… *Yuck*, I said at ten years old, but I remembered their martyrdoms forever.

Yet the one who came to mind most of all these days was the Blessed Virgin. She, of course, was not a saint suffering in the flesh, but the pure and radiant mother of Jesus. Eventually her entire body would be assumed into heaven, in fact. Mary taught me about the most exquisite pain of motherhood—not the anguish of childbirth, nor certainly any of the martyr's wounds. No, Mary's greatest painful moment for me was captured in the *Pietà*, her head bowed over her son's body. Being a mother of sons, I can't quite look at that sculpture without understanding what real agony is about.

There was one of Mary's roles I was especially fond of: *Stabat Mater Dolorosa*.[7]

The hymn envisions Mary's deep sorrows as stab wounds—beginning with the foreshadowing of her son's death in the temple, when Jesus was still a beautiful, brilliant boy who told her he must be about his father's business, to that greatest pain when she took her place at the bottom of the cross.

I imagined these and other torments as swords sticking out of Mary's chest. Each sorrow was a deep wound, like the gouge in my own. I loved that, and in my dreams and while they dressed my

---

[7]Stabat Mater Dolorosa, often referred to as Stabat Mater, is a 13th-century Catholic hymn to Mary, variously attributed to the Franciscan Jacopone da Todi and to Pope Innocent III. It is about the sorrows of Mary.

wound, I yearned for a doll made up that way, to remind me of what Mary, and so many mothers of sons, suffer.

I saw her as an ordinary single parent watching a football game and seeing her son James creamed on the two-yard line. A big knife through her heart. His failure to get into Washington and Lee—*Uhh, another blow.* David's heartbreak over that beauty queen from Ursuline School: *Oof, and another.* Mary had so many swords that when she walked, the weapons waved with her movement. She was *Stabby Mommy* in my dreams: you could hardly get near her for the swords sticking out.

How did she carry groceries? She must have ruined her bras. Where was I? I said, as I awakened in the hospital room one more day and saw the bevy of residents marching in with their clean, ready trays of bandages and their strained smiles.

While they worked on me, I would try to imagine what would be more horrible than this. I thought of Stabby Mommy and the grieving mothers. Bring on your tongs, your burning antiseptics, your surgical knives, and your probing fingers. Just don't let me sit there when they bring my boy back dead from Iraq and hand me that neatly folded flag.

Perhaps this explains my ongoing fondness for images of Mary, especially joined with my childhood vocation to be a Carmelite. (When I told my mother at age six that I wanted to join a community of women where nobody talked, she looked at me sourly and said, "Over my dead body.")

Although Ken's living room was filled with mostly Asian gods, there was one picture of the Blessed Mother in the china closet with the fancy plates. Perhaps Ken put her there as a concession to my Catholic upbringing, from parochial schools through high school and college at Mount Saint Agnes in Baltimore.

I thought of Mary frequently while I was in isolation, and asked Ken to bring a picture of her so I could tuck it into the drawer next to my hospital bed. He brought me a portrait of Mary and a companion picture of a suitable "sister" for the Virgin. The two make a special double portrait that gave me courage and reminded me of my fondness for nuns, my teachers from ages 5 to 21. As a child, I used to love to hold on to their skirts in the playground and smell the lavender soap of the cloth while I pushed away the oversize rosaries tied around their waists. My mother was called in by the superior a few months after my brother was born to be told that I was "starving for attention," and the good sisters, perhaps weary of my importunate hugs, advised her to give more affection to her five-year-old daughter.

The other, smaller, companion picture of a nun sitting at a desk reminded me of the power of feminism, and brought up some little pride in my own intellectual history. But, first, the other portrait.

Only seven inches in diameter, the larger portrait is a charming, round rendering of a lovely young girl dressed as an aristocrat. This is called an *escudo*, and is placed around the neck of the novice for the ceremony of taking her final vows. Created in 1783 in Mexico, the small exquisitely rendered painting on tin represents either the Blessed Mother or the novice, or maybe both. The family of the nun would pay for the creation of the *escudo*, its quality perhaps indicating the dowry of the young woman to the convent and the class esteem of the family.[8] The nun would actually wear it as she walked down the aisle. The face of the *escudo* portrait Ken brought me is exquisite, and I am enchanted by the delicate hands, and especially the pearls.

Pearls, you say? Delicious is the history of nuns who wear jewelry. Many wealthy women took the veil so that they would not have to be saddled with matrimonial and matriarchal duties. Instead, they

---

[8]Martha J. Egan, *Relicarios: Devotional Miniatures from the Americas* (Santa Fe, NM: Museum of New Mexico Press, 1993), especially 55–63, about the *escudos de monja,* the badges of nuns.

The Escudo painted on tin (1783) on top,
and Sor Juana Inés de la Cruz at her desk, circa 1675.

chose to live independently; in many convents, also comfortably. Most took their wealth with them into the community. Thus, characters like Chaucer's Prioress of the early fourteenth century in the *Canterbury Tales* had upper-crust manners and wore a necklace that said *"Amor Vincit Omnia."* Chaucer's winking irony in the jewelry reminding that "love conquers all" on one dedicated to chastity signals a culture where pearls could and did grace our Madonna or new nun with impunity.

And the smaller oval picture next to our bedecked lady may explain the possible origin of the *escudo*. Here is a gorgeous nun sitting in front of a desk with books behind her. This is no ordinary sister, but the fabulously brilliant Sor Juana Inés de la Cruz (1651–1695), self-taught scholar, acclaimed writer, and powerful advocate for women. More than a hundred years before the Mexican Madonna in our *escudo*, the bishops, seeing the vanity of the nuns who wore elaborate jewels to their final vows, forbade jewelry. Sor Juana may have been the one who suggested substituting the fancy brooches and necklaces of the rich novices for pious paintings of the Virgin to hang on the breast. Pictures of Sor Juana often show her wearing one, as this one does. And, in 1783 Mexico, for this *escudo*, the practice was still in use.

This small portrait of one of the most brilliant nuns from the Spanish Golden Age rallies my courage. I wrote the first feminist dissertation at the University of Maryland in 1977, and I know what challenging tradition feels like. And what it takes for a woman to create art. Joining a convent at 16, Sor Juana, in the seventeenth century, claimed this was the only way she would have time to express her talents; and express them she did! When the bishop ordered her to stick to religious topics in her writing, she proclaimed: "One can perfectly well philosophize while cooking dinner."

When I leaned over and opened my hospital drawer, the pictures of my two ladies soothed me and gave me a secret courage. There in these images was my childhood dream of being a nun translated into feminism; the necessity for shutting out the world sometimes to create my own art, and the enduring affection for Mother Mary.

CHAPTER SEVEN
WOUND

I lost 15 pounds in the first six weeks after the diagnosis of stage two breast cancer.

It was the early summer of 2007, and I had been in the hospital for nine days. I could still put my hair in pigtails then, before chemo. The oncologist, Dr. T, visited to give me the troublesome news that my BRCA1 gene score indicated a recurrence of cancer without chemo. Dr. T scheduled me for that treatment starting in July, just a few weeks later. I was losing weight by the day. Hospital food and worry were my diet. This was no way, said my oncologist, to prepare for chemo.

It was June 21, after nine days, five surgeries, constant IV drips, and many painful dressings, that I was finally sent home. It was clear now that I would need a mastectomy, but that would have to wait until after chemo was finished. At this point, I pushed aside the thought of future therapies and surgeries. I was most afraid, at that point, of the daily dressing of the breast wound.

The prospect frightened me because I would miss the interns and the residents. They were the ones who gazed at the horror every day. Now I would have to do it. Alone.

An angel appeared in the form of Rufae, a visiting nurse, who came to my co-op every day for the first week I was home. It was she who emboldened me to stand before the mirror, face the mutilated mound, and handle the medications and bandages. It was scrambled flesh, where the nipple used to be, a lumpy cavern, raw; a devil's mask. *Oh God,* I thought, *who would want to have sex with me? My life as a desirable woman is over.* Rufae would talk to me of healing, of the remarkable skills of plastic surgeons, of happy endings she had seen, tunnels with light. I held her big shoulders tight, let her go, and faced the mirror.

I was also eager to get back to seeing my psychologist. I had started this therapy in February of 2007, a few months before the diagnosis. It was time, I decided, to confront my lifelong issues with my mother. There was a long history of abuse, especially a violent temper, and I was exhausted with the emotional toll. Fortunately, she lived 1,500 miles away in Florida with my stepdad. As an adult, I gradually began to relate to her, even get along, mostly over the phone. I visited them in Florida, but only every few years.

In December 2006, just a few months before my cancer diagnosis, my stepdad, Paul, had an operation for colon cancer. In the weekly phone conversations, I heard my mother's fragility and worry about Paul. She needed a break from the caretaking. It had been a few years since I'd seen her, so I decided a short trip to see both of them was needed. So I flew to Orlando in January, and rented a car to drive to DeLand, an hour north of the airport.

Paul was in a rehab center after his cancer surgery, and I or Mom or both of us visited him every day. Paul, dubbed Paw Paw, was my stepdad, and had been my mother's husband for as long as she had been married to my biological dad—25 years. Mac, as my father was called, passed away in 1974 at 59. A gentle, dignified man, Paw Paw was very like my own father, with a remarkable ability to keep my mother content, and especially to manage her unpredictable rages. He seemed to be recovering nicely from the surgery, and for a few days all went well with the visit.

But then—a reprisal of my childhood traumas happened anyway, maybe because of his weakened influence on my mother. Another awful temper tantrum, this one in public. Mom became furious because I'd left her house for a few hours to run an errand in another town. When I returned, she said she needed to go to the grocery store up the street, but as soon as we got there, she started screaming at me that I was ungrateful. Then Mom, 85 years old, ran out of the store, with me running after her, and started pulling my hair in the parking lot, swinging me around the parked cars. The scene was so dramatic that a small crowd gathered, and one good Samaritan asked me if I wanted to call the police to calm her down. But by that time, Mom was exhausted and leaned against my car. I slowed my own breath and told the concerned woman that I was used to this and knew how to handle it. I got into the car and let Mom get in, then drove the few blocks back to her house, cringing against the driver's side, expecting another blow. But my mother was spent.

I remember as a child the wild beatings, mostly with yardsticks. I don't recall the physical pain as much as the emotional terror. I would be in bed in the dark when I was nine or ten, and suddenly the door would burst open to reveal her figure backlit from the overhead hall light. She would rush into the room, the yardstick raised, and begin to thrash me in the bed under the covers as she yelled, all the while bringing her fearsome face close to mine. The light from the hallway would reveal in mottled shadow her twisted mouth and bulging eyes. Even now, the conjuring of that fury chills my blood and speeds my heartbeat.

It was usually about something I forgot to do, or something I asked for which was too expensive, or which she thought was undeserved. Sometimes she would react immediately. My brother, a Hollywood screenwriter, laughs when he talks about how she was so full of fiery energy that her temper could turn anything into a verb.

"Mom, the girls at school are getting new blue blazers for Spirit Day," I would say in 8th grade. "Can we go to Hutzler's and see them, maybe?"

"I'll *blue blazer* you!" Mom proclaimed. My dad was a steamfitter, and we never knew when he'd bring home the white cartons of no-name CHEESE, LARD, and COFFEE—labeled in big letters—that the union provided instead of pay when there was no work. How could that man's child dare wish for such a glamorous garment?

"I'll blue blazer you" was the threat in colorful language; thank God, not the real thing—epic anger, ferociously focused, like a thrown grenade, aimed often at her daughter.

But her tantrums also lay in wait, like buried mines. You placed your feet carefully, watching your words, like the soles of battered boots on uneven sandy ground. Any step could trigger a possible explosion. Sometimes you'd reach the edge of the field with no incident, but you knew the explosives were there. And there were duds too.

It might have been hours before, when I had unwittingly omitted the action or said the awful, but the faulty bomb finally went off. There it was, Mom in the doorway backlit, raised weapon in hand and that mask of fury burned in place. Here was the nightmare image that made me understand post-traumatic stress syndrome.

Perhaps it is an insult to those who suffer the horrors of war and come back truly psychologically scarred, but I swear I understand. PTSD means a kind of mental flinch which triggers a small emotional tsunami. With only a suggestion of violence—a dark alley, unseen objects overhead (the yardstick), someone close behind, coming to a corner before the turn—I can slide into fear, anticipating physical harm. After repeated trauma I think there forms a dimple in the heart whose tiny cavern easily lets in the fear of danger. The dimpling force is, of course, a memory that won't die.

So that tirade in Winn-Dixie's parking lot with the gray-haired seniors as audience—their arms grasping grocery bags—became part of my recurring night sweats, born not of menopause but of nightmares in bed being ambushed by a … a mother? The ultimate protector? So, of course! Scary movies I eschewed. Give me a Disney animated film any time.

I had been terrified enough by real life.

What surprised me was my keen sense that this time on that mild Florida winter night, at 63, I would no longer put up with it.

Perhaps she sensed this, because Mom quieted down quickly in the short ride home, running into the house and then immediately into her bedroom, shutting the door almost gently.

Tremblingly determined, I packed my suitcase as quietly as I could. All those minutes, I expected her to come screaming into the room. But nothing, just the TV sounds from her room. I left the house in a half hour without saying goodbye, congratulating myself on courage under fire. At the local Walgreen's parking lot, a reward was calling my brother in California. I needed another witness besides the aging, open-mouthed neighbors.

Vince had been there in the bedroom next to mine when we were kids; he knew the years of furious scenes, her fists in the air; slamming me at the front door when I walked in a half hour late, tearing my clothes; later when I was a mother myself, her aborted visits to my single-parent home in New York, leaving suddenly because she felt slighted by one of my boyfriends; her white-hot madness over the phone during my pregnancy because her Mother's Day card did not arrive on time.

Vince, her only son, was clearly her favorite, but I didn't care. It was okay. He was a crucial witness anyway. I loved him deeply, the closest blood relative I had and have, before my sons. Our deep sibling

45

affection strained by geography and our mother's temperament is still a triumph of our growing up.

Growing up all I wanted to do was…

"Get the hell outta there! Do you need any money?" my brother almost shouted over the phone, echoing my constant wish growing up to get away from my mother.

That's when I broke down. Right there in front of Walgreen's sign for flu shots. Then, I knew I would get the hell out, once and for all, and I would never go through this again.

What took me so long? Checking my resistance to her, my rejection of her anger, were the memories of her intermittent and lopsided love. When, at 22, I left to teach US troops in Europe, she wrote to me every day for over a year. Her crooked handwriting on those APO-addressed envelopes showed up at whatever army or air force base I was moved to every eight weeks.

When Michael, my first husband, left me with a two-month-old and a three-and-a-half-year-old, she flew to New York a few days later, distraught and furious at him, but she was there. After two weeks, she begged me to let her go back to her husband, my stepdad, threw tantrums against my departed husband in front of my sons, and vomited in the living room after yet another migraine. I released her back to Florida with thanks on many levels. But she came to me when my abandonment was raw and bleeding. And, most of all, in the first years after Michael left, she and Paul brought us to Jacksonville at Christmas, taking us to treats I couldn't afford, like Sea World and Typhoon Land and Disneyland. During the year, Mom would research the fun to come for her grandsons, becoming a divining rod for every cockamamie attraction within driving distance (chauffeured by the long-suffering Paul): the ancient fort in St. Augustine; miniature golf in a dragon park; the snake museum in Debary; a place featuring turtle races; a big wooden statue of an Indian chief that made my mother laugh; the sea in winter. We put up the Christmas tree like a family. I got to nap whenever I wanted. David ate broccoli for his grandma. Paw Paw taught them manly things, like marine knots, or how to drive a nail or a motorboat.

But tonight—the night of the parking lot hair-pulling—it had been years since those distant kindnesses.

My mother lived in DeLand, a college town hugging Stetson University. I remembered a small hotel next to the campus. After an hour in a waspy wine bar, dousing my sorrows in Cabernet and watching pretty sophomores chat, I had a quick burger and headed for the modest inn. It was good to walk into the Green Awning Lodge, where I slept badly in the Lysol-aromatic bedroom. The next morning, I drove the rental car—thank God I rented a car this time and didn't use my mother's—to the Orlando airport.

Back home, it is a few weeks later and I am driving to see my new psychotherapist. A friend recommended Dr. Michael S when I related the Florida story in the context of shared parental complaints. "She did what?" said my friend. After a brief conversation on the phone, I decided to try out this dude. Michael was eager to deal with my allowing Mom's abuse for so many years. Why did I put up with it? Some serious defect in my character needed to be fixed.

Then, after two months of this therapy theme, I was diagnosed with breast cancer. So between my apparent masochism and the breast cancer, we had plenty to talk about. Every other Wednesday evening became my shrink night.

SIDE EFFECTS

CHAPTER EIGHT
COMPANY

Cancer patients, according to at least one famous study, are more likely to survive if they belong to a support group. Michael told me that. But I recoiled from a group of strangers. Besides, Michael was always more interested in my being *authentic,* of protecting myself from the wants of others so I could fully be. I am trying to get that.

No fainting couch for me. I sit across from Michael in an upright leather chair. The light is turned down so that he appears to be coming at me from out of the shadows, as if we are in a noir movie starring Alan Ladd in a trench coat.

Michael: "What did you think about that description of the 'other person directedness' I gave you last week?"

"Uh, what does it mean again?"

Michael almost smirked with disapproval. Little puffs of that emerged when I wasn't on topic. I could see the gap between his front teeth, which made him look like Alfalfa, one of the characters from *The Little Rascals*, from my TV youth.

"Other-directedness means that the needs of others trump the needs of self. The self becomes subordinated," he said.

"God, a dead ringer for me… Others… surrendering control… conditional love. That's Mom's thing. 'You better be good,' she'd snarl, 'or I'll wipe the floor up with you.'"

Michael is small and slight, with tight curly auburn hair and intense eyes. Once he told me he practiced the jazz guitar six hours a day. You can feel the music locked up inside of him. I know that type. Years ago I lived with a classical guitarist who loved alcohol more than he loved me. I had to finally send him away, but I would gladly hear again the early-morning *pavannes* he played with tenderness and those long fingernails.

I like it that Michael is in shadow. It is easier for me to cry, or to be angry. Like the poet, John Donne, said, "Churches are best for prayer that have least light." This was one of my chapels of survival, I suppose.

I saw Michael every other week that spring and summer, except when I was in the hospital recovering from E. coli. When I saw him after the hiatus, I was hungry for his response. It was just a few days after my discharge, and I had poured out my heart about the ordeal. Soon I would begin chemo, and I confessed my dread. My message was, "*I have already gone through enough, but there is much more ahead. Sympathy, I need big-time sympathy!*"

But Michael is more concerned with my being "real" than my living through cancer and its side effects. He is always telling me that the purpose of life is to be true to yourself, once you know the self, of course. It doesn't really matter if you have one or two breasts, or whether your ticket has already been punched for the other side.

He gets impatient with me when I want to talk about the books I love or even my dreams, and so the music dies a little. Michael wants me to know that all my life I have had an excessive focus on the desires, feelings, and responses of "others, at the expense of one's own needs." He repeats it for impact.

Awful results follow from this self-sacrifice. I give too much of me away. Sometimes I don't even know if I like something or not (is that why I feel that way about LinkedIn?). And it all comes from a mother who ignored or punished my real self.

My mom probably "beat the authenticity out of me," Michael says.

All this seems approximately true, but how is it helpful NOW? I stare at the odd drawings behind his head, and wonder if he gets much sex.

SIDE EFFECTS

CHAPTER NINE
GIRLFRIENDS

What are friends for, my mother asks.
A duty undone, visit missed,
Casserole unbaked for sick Jane.
Someone has just made her bitter.

Nothing. They are for nothing, friends,
I think. All they do in the end—
They touch you. They fill you like music.
~ Rosellen Brown

It is the day after the first chemo treatment, and side effects are weeks away. I am feeling good. I have, after all, survived the infection and the hospital, and even the frightening first day at Dr. T's sanctum sanctorum. So I decide to take a run on Eagle Valley Road where Ken's house sits—a big red renovated 19th century barn ensconced in country style—on blind curves and with no sidewalk. It is a fun road for driving, but dicey for walking. Still, I am happy, so happy to see my sneakered foot fall on the blend between grass and macadam, smell the fullness of woods in July, and be fully alive on the street where I mostly live now, and where my love lives.

I rejoice in the individualized houses—some old, some refurbished, some clearly 1950s, each distinct, as if elbowing its neighbor, saying,

"I am next to, but not *like* you!" Often, there are deep back yards I long to enter. One place has a van: *Mobile Doggie Salon*; another announces the storkdelivery.com—slivers of American enterprise. A couple of rough-and-tumble trucks for sale. There is a sort of New Orleans house, colorful and flowerpot-laden; some others with messy English gardens; or the one with a gigantic weeping willow, branches like eyelashes over the gaze of a front porch. Or, there's our neighbor's home with a huge swath of rolling lawn announcing a brown-shingled mansion, a serious facade despite the giggle of a basketball hoop. Another hundred yards and there, atop a little rise, is a 24-hour chapel with the sign "Blessed Sacrament Present," next to the church named for St. Joan of Arc. Plants at my moving feet, morning air, a solitary country road, the poetry of dwellings that tell of those who have survived crises too, like I will, I say to myself; those who are having their coffee while I run by, curious and respectful, and chastened by life, but blessed.

The peaceful aloneness of the run reminded me about therapy and Michael's bugging me about a support group.

I knew that I needed others around me, but I didn't want an institutional group. I found my support everywhere—healthy friends, sick ones, distant ones, those so close they handled my wounds, phone friends, card-sending friends, friends who were resentful, curious friends, friends who had been there, work friends, prayer friends, and one friend in a book. I made a deal with Michael that I would find my support group and ask them for what *I NEEDED*. Authenticity could surely be sharpened when you were poised for death.

It was my girlfriends who were the great bastions of the fortress that protected me from death.

As I ran that summer day, I thought of the dinner party a few weeks before.

Diane was General Patton. A fierce soldier with glamour.

It was late June on Diane's stone-tiled veranda, shaded by 100-year-old trees. Hors d'oeuvres on Mexican plates, brightly patterned napkins. A circle of women lounged on cushioned deck chairs. Our hostess handed out copies of a calendar with all my chemo dates marked in red.

Diane: Everyone have a pen? Now who can take Carole to her next treatment—July 14?

Joanie raised her hand.

Diane: Does that work for you, Joanie? Good. Can you take her and bring her back?

Lyuba: I can come get her after school. About 4 o'clock?

Diane: Closer to 5, I think. It's a six-hour treatment.

Carole: I don't want anyone waiting for me that long...

Diane: Don't be silly. It's one day. That's why we are sharing the work. Lyuba, that's good. Joan can do it earlier and then go to pick up her grandson.

Writes on the calendar.

Diane: Dene, can you take her on July 21?

Dene: No, I'm in camp. But I will take her downtown to that surgeon she wants to consult; you know, about the ... uh, breast surgery, cosmetic thing.

Diane: We don't yet know the details about her surgery. But, OK... I'll reserve you for a downtown trip.

I was silent, looking at each face I knew so well. I watched while they circled dates and noted times. The floral plate on my lap blurred a little when I looked down, and I quickly shoved a cracker in my mouth to squelch emotion.

Phone calls were also scheduled to check up on me. I had rides to Ken's house in the country on weekends. Wig shopping? *I will go with you.* How about the farmer's market—Diane's favorite—to buy organic. *I'll drive you to the one in Bronxville. No! I'll go for you, and bring you peaches and strawberries.* How will she get to the train station next week? She has a special test at Sloan. *Me! I can do that.* What do you need for food, for medicine? *WE will be there.*

And so it went, with each woman piping up with their offering.

Diane put a last scribble on the calendar. With that, she swooped up the plate of hummus from the picnic table and asked, "Who needs more wine?"

Before we knew it, she was serving us a gourmet dinner in her antique dining room: osso bucco over pappardelle pasta, and this delicacy offered after marshaling eight women and their calendars for the next four months.

As they raised their glasses to me, I made them drink first, as I turned the toast back to them and their giving hearts. I prayed to myself that I would live long enough to return their generosity. And we dined in that loving atmosphere!

The figure of Diane, her proud posture, her talents of organization, communication, culinary arts, fashion, marketing and diplomacy, her physical beauty and stunning style—these composed her arsenal in my defense against the weakness, fear, and despair. Once she strode into my hospital room, in her hand a cobalt blue bottle with one perfect peony. This was what health looked like, and I yearned for it. Her strength of purpose to help me in any way she could, roused me and attracted others.

Her shining moment was early on in the big crisis—the emergency room in Sound Shore where she came back and forth from her home with fresh gourmet sandwiches; steady, reasonable indignation; and compassionate listening. Throughout, she was a stable, unhurried witness of the crisis. No panic, just there for me while I figured it out. Her coolness in the midst of wild worry, pain, and confusion was a serene hand on my forehead.

Others gave what they could. What they could bear, what suited their talents. Who was the saint who wanted to give God a gift, but all he had was his talent of juggling? So he juggled before the Lord and received favor. I learned to celebrate the many gifts of love. Dene was the driver par excellence. Lyuba brought me a funny sculpture of a hand with fingers crossed—it taught me once more about fickle fortune, about laughter. Mynetta kept my job going for me and shepherded the avalanche of e-mails from well-wishers. Joan pressed spiritual books on me as well as her cheerful, relentless phone calls. Mary reminded me to go easy with sharing the details about my ordeal. "This is really hard on me," she complained on the phone one night—she was in Baltimore, five hours away—"Your being sick is a terrible stress to deal with." Barbara gave me goji berries and pursued alternative medicine research. Rose had her husband, a dentist, make me an expensive dental device which helped me sleep easier. The nurses, especially the visiting nurse who came to my home, gave me the courage to face the terrible wound and dress it myself. It was a courage I returned to over and over again.

Dene, Lyuba, Mynetta, Mary, Joan, Barbara, Rose, Rufae…

Their support felt like the metaphor I used with my sophomore classes at the University of Maryland. Teaching Sophocles's *Oedipus*, I tried to show the archetypal struggle to do the right thing, to hold on to the good against the inexorable Fate which had doomed him to kill his father and marry his mother. I asked my students to see a wind tunnel in which Oedipus walked against his destiny and the force of the gale. I asked the class to see handles along the tunnel that Oedipus grasped as he pushed his way ahead. It wasn't the most hopeful metaphor. Destiny, after all, creamed Oedipus. But the fact that he tried was the heroic part that moved us to pity and also awe, that made Oedipus's story more than just a sad event. I also needed to feel heroic during chemo, the many operations, and the dark nights. Help from others felt like a signal from another force going the other way from cancer, my healthy friends' gestures—those weary voices on the phone asking, "How ya doing?" and their wan smiles at the end of their workday as they drove me to the oncologist felt like those handles in the wind tunnel. They offered me the chance for slow progress—somewhere different, somewhere hopeful—as I bent against the wind.

CHAPTER TEN
CHEMO

Another source of strength, the comfort of company, was the sick group—patients at the oncologist's office who sat in those Barcaloungers in a lime green room no bigger than a large bedroom. Ten-foot-high machines, computers, and rolling stools, a metal forest, interrupted nurses and aides weaving in and out among the eight or nine patients in the room. There was an attempt to arrange the loungers in a rough circle so we could see one another between the wires, metal arms, and IVs. The cancer patients in chemo are not necessarily great conversationalists. The culture of the waiting room spills over here, but when they do share, there is comfort. Perhaps it is because of the slight bedroom ambience. A sign might have said: "DOZING ALLOWED HERE."

Company in the chemo room was a pastel version of the movie, *Dead Man Walking*, I thought at first. Women with scarves and awful pink sweatshirts with encouraging sayings; sometimes a silent man with a computer watching a movie; women with hats; women with wigs; women covered by blankets, afghans; all with bottles next to them and the dripping medicine. Half human, half machine, we reclined obediently, pillows under our bald heads, our hats over bald heads, or good or bad wigs.

Here we took Adriamycin, Cytoxsin, Taxol, Herceptin, and 20 other kindly poisons dripping into our veins, our ports, our hands, our arms—depending on what aperture would accept yet another IV. I dreaded the port—a two-inch incision made in the upper chest with a permanent opening for intravenous fluids. You had to have a port if your veins became calcified, shrunken, or invisible. It was a kindly intervention: a little window in the flesh for them to access your bloodstream easily, but I would gladly suffer the digging needle to avoid a hole in my chest.

I had always had big, easy veins, but after a week or so of Cytoxsin, I found my blood highways shrinking against the chemicals. It was hard to find a welcoming opening, as if the veins learned to retreat from the terrible onslaught of poison armies. They were unwilling, poor dears, to be traitors to my natural health, but too weak against the strong medicine.

Maybe that's why nurses in chemo labs are the best phlebotomists in the world. They deal with condemned veins every day, so they are the premier prospectors. You watch their eyes as they assess the possibilities in your elbow or your upper arm. They turn the limb, their thumbs grasping the forearm, with a sad and experienced eye. You know you are disappointing them, and your heart sinks even before the drip of toxins. These oncology nurses are falcons of blood rivers, Hawkeyes of embattled flesh, and seekers of desert gulches that might yield tiny runs into the system. All the time they know they are hurting you, that you can only stand the deep pricking so much. The threat of a port that will require surgery and another scar to remind you of cancer hovers over their hands, eyes. Aha—they find a vein, this time in your hand. It hurts like hell, but it is staving off the port, so you can count on someday wearing a strapless dress and not having a scar that says, "I had chemo and they needed to do this to get in." *How ridiculous*, I thought. *I'm facing several operations on my breast, and I'm worried about a couple of spoiled inches next to my shoulder bone!* Still, I loved the nurse that told me, "I will get you through." We both knew what she meant: "I will keep you from getting a surgical port for the next four months, if I possibly can. I WILL FIND A VEIN, goddamit."

We loved the aide called Gina. She was an ex-cop, probably a lesbian, with a big tattoo on her left calf. Easily 180 lbs., with a short dark haircut, smooth skin, and the kind of face that could be beautiful if not for its willful simplicity and strength. But she had a comedian's talent, the perfect timing of remarks:

"Who has to pee? I can only take one at a time. In the meantime, I am selling lollipops: strawberry, cherry, and this green thing. We have a run on cherry. And you, you take the green because I had to get up twice to unlock you to pee…"

She talked of her vacation going to Foxwoods, Atlantic City, for gambling, supporting the Indians because "we robbed them of their land. I gotta make it up to them." She mentioned her swimming pool with her dog who often almost drowned; her naughty demanding nephews, her silly neighbors, and her own health problems, an arthritis which marked her a teetotaler and plagued her with incessant pain.

Our feet pointed to the center of the room, leaving a circle and a fringe of shoes and socks for Gina, an area that gave her an ersatz stage. We watched her in the middle of us sorting bandages, listened to her impromptu complaints, her bravado challenges to the boss nurses. Our weak smiles focused on her next remark in a sick room Vegas act that always worked. "Wanna go home? When the nurses aren't looking, I'll squeeze your IV bags so you can finish quicker." Gina was most popular when the nurses were finding a vein. We grabbed for her humor and avoided the searching fingers on our arms.

Those chemo friends I met here I did not take home with me. But there was one I followed for some time, even after our treatment time together. She spoke to a special need, yet she was very different from me. For one thing, she was from another social class.

I met Carolyn in the middle of my treatment. I knew she was rich the moment I saw her checking in at the desk in the oncologist's waiting room. Her wig was expensive, for one thing. I was proud of my $39 versions, which I found in Mount Vernon and New Rochelle. I bought three wigs before I lost one hair. I thought I would have variety while I was sick, and then afterward, I told my friends, I'd be set to rob banks. One wig was for Tina Turner—brown with long blonde streaks; it reached my shoulders and gave me sexy bangs; another was like Uma Thurman in *Pulp Fiction*—short reddish brown with a close-cropped back and longer sides that graced my face nicely—my "work wig," I called it. Then there was one Mynetta got me—long black hair, sort of an Addams Family look, but modified. For parties, I thought, my stomach queasy with the thought of healthy people eating and drinking. Finally, there was the short platinum blonde one for $29. I bought it from an earnestly sympathetic Korean woman in a local shop. She was encouraging, but it turned out the wig was too small; it slowly rode up on my head, so I was constantly pulling it down around my ears. The Marilyn wig, as I called it, was great with pink lipstick, and it distracted from my absent eyelashes. I ended up spending $60 to have it made bigger by a hairdresser who worked for the Metropolitan Opera.

But Carolyn's wig was gorgeous. She paid several thousand for it, and it looked so real, I was surprised when she told me it was a wig. Still, she felt she had to wear a baseball cap over it. In her 40s, Carolyn had discovered an aggressive form of cancer a year before during a breast augmentation operation. Only 2 percent of the population had such a serious version of the disease. She was undergoing chemo and would have further surgery afterward. I liked Carolyn's quiet beauty and her courage in the face of such a serious prognosis. Her youth touched me, as did her devoted husband, Fred, who, despite her surgery, still looked at her with a barely disguised passion.

But it was her 9-year-old daughter who took my breath away. She came to see her mother during one treatment, and I fell in love with this little sprite, with her sweet energetic body and her mother's dark eyes. At 63, it was hard to lose a breast, to suffer, to face the possibility of death; but at 43, it was harder. My boys were on their way at 24 and 28, but Carolyn's daughter clearly needed her and would for some time. When we talked during treatment, I mothered Carolyn as much as I could. She, in turn, gave me admiration and consolation in a deeper way than anyone else.

I'm not sure why we connected, but I felt we were going somewhere together. Indeed, she had her first breast surgery just a few weeks before I did. Those phone conversations both grounded and emboldened me for the ordeal ahead. I guess I needed from Carolyn the knowledge that my condition could be worse. I lost touch with Carolyn after my own surgery months later, but her company was a gift of the chemo experience. Of all those I met, however, I worry most about recurrence for Carolyn. Her youth, the intensity of her disease, signaled that strong possibility. I pray that I am wrong, but I cannot call her today.

Another treasured companion was one book, only one. With years of professional reading behind me, one would think I would find solace in many different volumes. After all, I was an old English teacher, at last fairly free of the marketplace of work and with time on my hands. A paradise of reading, *n'est-ce pas?* Besides the classics I missed or read too rapidly for the doctoral gauntlet of dozens of courses, papers, and brutal three-hour comprehensives, books like *Remembrance of Things Past*, there were all the inspiring, absorbing written journeys of survivors. The literature about and for breast cancer would paper the walls of a commodious chapel. From *First You Cry* (1980) to the most recent hilarious romps by sassy young ladies in the grip of stage four. Then, my doctors and friends showered me with cheerful diagrams of breast reconstruction and straightforward explanations of treatments and what to expect with reasonable confidence. There were books meant to be spiritual buttresses, arias about positive thinking, little stories that were the psychic equivalents of cups of chicken soup to the one with the cancerous or lost breast. But whether it was the purported brain addling of chemo or just my restless spirit, I couldn't read this stuff.

After 10 minutes of perusal, I would put the book next to my bed. In a few months, a leaning tower of hopeful dog-eared tomes reached from floor to lamp base.[9]

There was one exception. Mark Nepo's *Surviving Has Made Me Crazy*[10] grabbed me by the throat and would not let me go. Nepo had an aggressive form of lymphoma, brain tumors, four months of chemo, and surgery removing another malignant tumor from his chest. He had the smackdown of the death sentence and survived, only to be thrust back on the mat again. Writing from the vantage point of 12 years of being cancer free, but still wary, he released me from the feminine lament. He gave me poetry with a virile voice:

---

[9] Yet here I am writing a breast cancer survivor memoir and asking my reader to do what I could not do! Later I read *Cancer Schmancer* by Fran Drescher and *Why I Wore Lipstick to My Mastectomy*. Perhaps I wasn't sure that my story would end as happily, and didn't want to read about a success which might elude me. Mark Nepo, being a man, was so different from me, and I loved his vigor!

[10] Originally published 2007, by CavanKerry Press. His poems affirm that surviving has more to do with authenticity than with our longevity, a theme that also captured my heart. Nepo is a teacher, poet, and spiritual guide; and he continues to inspire, comfort, and enlighten about how sacred and useful everything is.

"Everyone is after me to stay positive, but/ tonight I feel like pissing on a rock."

I identified with his surgery. His chest was opened to remove a cancerous rib. I knew what it was to have an infected breast removed, what it was like to be cut, to have parts taken away.

Cancer, for Nepo, can sometimes show us the "face of God," but it is also brutal. "We also live like burn survivors screaming at the air." Nepo was honest company, teaching me that illness like this brands your soul as well as your body; it *transmogrifies.* My favorite book whispering at my bedside was this kindly, scared, and scarred guide who showed me that suffering could be a ticket to wisdom, even to joy.

A universe of company surrounded me, concentric circles of company expanding outward—from healthcare providers, to chemo buddies I knew over four months, to special friends like Diane and Mynetta, to Ken, to my friend in Baltimore who called me faithfully and frequently, to other colleagues from work, to my sons and family in California, more distant phone friends all over the country, to professional counselors, to my mom who was working hard to keep my stepdad alive and could not handle also visiting me here, to the angels, to the Holy Ghost, to the Blessed Mother. Even to the Sacred Heart himself—His coronary open to the world; the throbbing heart of Jesus, bloody big, flaming, and out there. With that colorful, wide-open chest, He sure seemed like a friend of mine.

And collapsing inward to me in the middle of the night—the concentric circles of my company—in my bed at home, in my hospital beds, in the chemo room waking from a tiny nap and seeing the drip in my arm, waiting in some doctor's examining room, in the awful claustrophobia of the CT scan, in solitary walks on Eagle Valley Road, in numerous churches and chapels, in the front passenger seat in cars, in many bathrooms, on many toilets, over many sinks, I was alone, completely alone—facing the cruel truth of now and hunting with my clawing fingers for my faith in the future. Despite all the kindness and vigor of my company's compassion, their urgency to save me, I knew they might very well fail.

CHAPTER ELEVEN
KEN

The Sea of Faith
Was once, too, at the full, and round earth's shore
Lay like the folds of a bright girdle furl'd.
But now I only hear
Its melancholy, long, withdrawing roar,
Retreating, to the breath
Of the night-wind, down the vast edges drear
And naked shingles of the world.

Ah, love, let us be true
To one another! for the world, which seems
To lie before us like a land of dreams,
So various, so beautiful, so new,
Hath really neither joy, nor love, nor light,
Nor certitude, nor peace, nor help for pain;
And we are here as on a darkling plain
Swept with confused alarms of struggle and flight,
Where ignorant armies clash by night.
~ Matthew Arnold, "Dover Beach"

Ken and I were together many nights in the country, where dawn came in gracefully through ancient tree limbs and lightening meadows. But there were those mornings when I woke solitary in my Mount Vernon co-op, and the first sound I heard at 6 a.m. was the klickety-klack of the custodian's cart outside on the pavement three floors below.

Carmelo, the kindly custodian who spoke the most baffling Spanish-accented English, a sound which matched the cart, was starting his day—with a rusty broken thing carrying his tools. The wheels were steel, not rubber, and one was warped, so the cart rattled and grated terribly when he dragged it over the concrete pavement. It was salmon colored like a fish, and every morning Carmelo yanked it from the outdoor shed to the basement, a 100-foot path under my bedroom window. It was more reliable than the rooster announcing the dawn, and infinitely more saddening.

When I was sick, that sound banished whatever dream of health I floated in, and announced instead the reality of my day with cancer, the terrible blandness of the doctors' offices, the needle, the strange rashes, the endless pills, the thin look of my hairless eyes in the mirror, the side effects of staying alive. The bumps of Carmelo's ramshackle cart were my version of Matthew Arnold's "melancholy, long, withdrawing roar" he made us hear in "Dover Beach." Instead of the sea and the "night wind, down the vast edges drear/and naked shingles of the world," there was the complaint of old wheels on a broken journey, and the existential slap of being alone.

When I heard that cart, I wanted Ken there so I could turn to him and say, "Ah, love, let us be true to one another."

But in those days, Ken was not often there in my apartment.

The truth was that this man I loved was not good with sick people. Although he went to medical school in the 1970s and mastered the academic learning necessary to be a thoracic surgeon, he never practiced medicine; he never embarked on a residency.

Second century Gandhara Buddha, restored

"In the rounds in the hospital, I could answer the questions at the bedsides," Ken said. "But with the patients, I could feel the energy being drained out of me. Ultimately, I couldn't stand it, and had to leave."

What he could do was translate his scientific skills, maybe even his compassion, to art. Ken was a master conservator of sick paintings, broken sculpture, and ruined artifacts. Over the years, he grew to be a premier conservator, and even a professor at NYU, on the materials of art. Able to fix the damage with an apparently magic touch, Ken became the physician who could heal the wounds to beauty.

I learned this one night when, early in our courtship, I stayed with him in the master bedroom at the country house. One night I got up to go to the bathroom and, because there was less light than I was used to, I ran into the ancient stucco Gandharan Buddha that stood next to the door. There was an awful crash, and when Ken turned on the light I saw, to my horror, the head broken and the rest of the body smashed. All over the carpet was mere dust and tiny pieces, like part of his hand, and, Oh God, most of his nose. We would have to vacuum up this god! I became a little hysterical until Ken told me he would fix it in the morning, and to please go back to sleep.

The next day I stayed in the kitchen nervously fixing what I hoped was a compensatory breakfast, trying not to hear the Hoover sucking up this precious relic from the second century. *Ha,* I thought, *this accident is beyond thousands of dollars. I am doomed to make amends to this god of peace and Eastern wisdom.*

An hour passed with no Ken in sight. Then he called me upstairs to his laboratory and I was astonished to see surely ANOTHER statue. There before me was an even more beautiful Buddha, his halo or penumbra behind him only half revealed (Ken said he didn't like the full one anyway), and the break and glue marks invisible. My gifted surgeon of the arts fashioned a nose, a finger, and sanded down the lost chunks from the shattering. Although I hadn't much noticed the original piece, I was sure that this one was more stunning, more dignified and graceful, the god with his hand over his robes and his third eye staring at me. The Buddha had been reincarnated under Ken's skilled hand.

After I kissed and hugged him, squealing with delight, he said he did it because now, perhaps, I would not suffer the wrath of the god for my bungling pee trip, and I would be less likely to come back in the next life ... as a cockroach.

As for my ordeal with breast cancer, Ken was not so good at sympathizing, but he did confront one side effect with a gusto that almost obliterated its sting: hair loss.

Initially, I had the typical hopes of the chemo patient: my hair wouldn't fall out. I would be different. I would cling to the odd story, "That lady has kept her hair for six sessions!" Then reality hit. Yep, hit me square in the head.

It was the second chemo treatment, the day after. I was blow-drying my hair. When I rolled it around the brush, the entire lock just eased out, from the scalp to the ends. No pain, just a release of the fistful of hair. It felt like what the Renaissance love poets say about orgasm: "a little death." But this letting go was not sexy. Ken heard me cry out, and came into the bathroom to say:

"Today is the day we shave your head."

I was so distracted that I didn't notice he was talking in a very good German accent.

He disappeared for a few minutes and returned with a battered box, ushering me into the kitchen with a towel. He pulled out some rusty clippers, an old pair he had used on his now deceased pet, a Shih Tzu named Toasty.

(Later, much later, he told me that he used to shave Toasty's anus when it got dirty and matted from doggie pooping.)

But then he went into action. With a relentless Nazi patter and an awful tenderness, Ken tucked my head under his arm and aimed the clippers.

"Could you (*sob*) make it like a half-inch long all over?" I squeaked.

"Nein! I only do this one way when I am prepar-ying ze victim for the showers. Das ist clean! We make it cleeeeen, like za bowling ball."

"Oh, Ken, you are so non-PC! This is hard enough." Tears and giggles mingling.

"You vill like it. You vill zee in the mirror ... you will look like a little boy. Those lousy French say the word. . . ."

"You mean, *gamin*?" I muttered, staring at my dyed blonde locks on the floor.

And then it was over.

While Ken swept up the hair, I finally had the courage to peer into the small kitchen mirror by the front door. The tiny reflection showed me a creature from another planet—big eyed and gentle looking, with a well-shaped head and small, shell-like ears. Almost lovely, but strange. I came close to the image and said, "Nefertiti?" and Ken nodded over the broom. I rubbed the top of my head and felt the tickle of the buzz cut. It felt so cool on this hot August day. An odd delight flowed through me, and surprise: like a baby emerging from the struggle of the womb, seeing smiles in the new world. I ran into the bathroom to get a better look. *Hey, is this me?*

When I took a shower to get rid of the errant hairs, the pleasurable feel of the water on my head made me laugh out loud. Oh, I would use lots of eye makeup and dangling earrings all the time and chokers on my long neck and put on lip gloss incessantly. I would perfume my scalp so that when I moved, fragrance would encircle me. And I would be an oddball beauty!

Much later, when my hair grew to my shoulders, my friends would pout and say, "We liked you bald; we loved you bald."

In bed that night, Ken told me he found the bald head sexy. I thought as much, for when he put his hand on my head, he seemed to get more excited than usual. *The androgynous look turns him on! Or is he secretly gay? Shave my head and make me a boy for his pleasure. Icky? Or kinky?* Then he also told me about the women he knew when he worked at Macy's: on his subway commute, bald twins he loved to look at. Although they were not young, they were strikingly beautiful. Very thin, model thin; with high cheekbones and a flair for big bracelets and *haute couture*. They would sometimes dye their scalps different colors to match their outfits. Blue and pink and green. Ken never spoke to them, a good way to stay bewitched.

"Baldness makes you more beautiful and different. You look like an artist," he whispered. "Your face is ovoid, and having no hair emphasizes its shape—thinner and more exotic, like your friend, Diane."

SIDE EFFECTS

CHAPTER TWELVE
SEX

Trying to be sultry while your body is breaking down under chemo is humbling: in the front was my ravaged right breast, which I had to cover with a tight tee-shirt and maybe a little padding to disguise the diminished and mutilated shape. But then I had what appeared to be a herpes breakout—a new affliction apparently caused by a breakdown in my immune system—on my ass, so I couldn't turn away demurely to hide the breast. In addition, my big toe had lost a nail to some infection, so it was covered with a large band-aid. The baldness was the least of my cosmetic problems. No eyelashes to bat either. My right shin had developed a bulbous red tumor-like thing above my ankle. Trying to hide all these flaws and still give a come-hither look was like being in Cirque du Soleil with no tricks. I just twisted myself, showing brief glimpses of whatever body part I had that was not warped or bandaged or lumpy or infected, and hoped for the best. Ken again surprised me: he just rubbed the top of what he called my "nappy" head, enfolded me in his arms, and gave me a warm and passionate kiss on my still perfect mouth.

Yes, Ken could be quite cool at times when I wanted to complain about side effects—his *patientphobia* set in. So I railed and wept with my therapist, Michael, or called my girlfriends. I did not share my pain with Ken. But often he would give me something stronger than sympathy. He reminded me that there was a life beyond illness.

Once, when he found me trying to hide my tears, he brought me a large wooden box. Inside was a remarkable book, so fat with stitched flowers and leaves that it barely closed. Here I discovered C. K. Lownds, who lived through the Civil War and was even writing in this book's final pages in 1896, during what must have been her last years.

Miss C. K. Lownds knew Harriet Beecher Stowe, lived in New York and Connecticut most of her life, and memorialized occasions with meticulously mounted botanicals. Each leaf or flower or stem was surrounded by exquisitely tiny handwriting explaining the provenance: "the Kimble's anniversary party," or "from Baby Mami's funeral." At the end of her life, in this precious book, she wrote poetry about loneliness and the missing of warm smiles. It would seem irresistible to see Miss Lownds as an old maid whose life's purpose was to record other people's occasions, but her book became more than that to me.

I imagined her head bent over a delicate piece of greenery, capturing in needle pricks a remnant from the funerals of the Civil War. One page held a piece of the cloth that draped the flag over Lincoln's coffin. Others gave us relics of happier times, of anniversary parties, marriages of cousins and neighbors. More than one posy remembered "Sanitary Fairs" where patriotic friends joined to wrap bandages for the Civil War soldiers. I see her putting into her pocket a bud no one would miss, and spending her youth carefully giving it a kind of immortality in sepia-infused mementos. A sort of botanical Emily Dickinson, C. K. Lownds and her handiwork brought me out of my depression about being what I felt I was—a female Job: full of the side effects of chemo, scarred by cancer; and frightened of the next affliction.

At least I had lived beyond the restrained sphere of Miss Lownds. I was relishing my own rich life, with all its dangers, and not

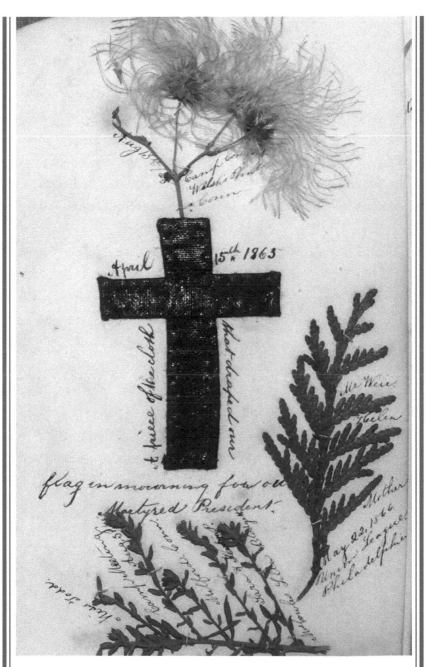

The cross, in Lownds' words, "is a piece of the cloth that draped our flag in mourning for our martyred President." Perhaps her most spectacular memento mori.

somebody else's. Was her world only recorded in crucified flowers from another's occasion, or was her inner life a rich landscape of savored emotion from the least of God's creations? After all, she was touching me over 150 years later, lifting me into her own lapidary imagination, literally with her hands and passion.

As I sniffed and dried my eyes over the pages, growing calmer as I examined each page, there came a more dazzling thought. Just as Ken gave me this oddly tender book to soothe me, Lownds made this to comfort herself. It was her way, perhaps, of lifting herself out of despair.

And this book will survive beyond Lownds's life, even beyond my life. And if it is cared for, preserved, and cherished, as all works of art should be, it will last for others to look at and be amazed, and maybe be comforted too. Nature, which conquered Lownds's body and will conquer mine, is caught in her labors as art. Beauty has been fashioned here through her patient fingers and relentless eye.

So many others will give me, through the healing arts, the relief from pain that I long for, but Ken's works of art will give me the joy of beauty, Through it, I hold hands with a long line of others who have marveled and will marvel at Lownds's book and other beautiful things—despite death, despite pain, despite cruelty—and take care of those wonders so that the next generation, and the next, can go on loving them down through time.

CHAPTER THIRTEEN
TASTE

When wiggling through a hole
The world looks different than
When scrubbed clean by the wiggle
And looking back.
~ Mark Nepo

A fter a few weeks on Adriamycin…
Chemo is an opportunist and a sadist, who will look for all weaknesses and pounce. He is a bully and generally uncreative. Chemo is a puritan in regard to sexual hunger, capacity, and lubrication. He also loves to make you look the opposite of romantic, robbing you of cranial hair, eyelashes, eyebrows.

Chemo is a terribly demanding culinary fiend, tending to the anorexic in my case. Unoriginal, bland, and favoring white food, like bread or bananas, he emaciates you so you know who's in control. Chemo hates the mouth in general, preferring to have you suck on what seem like pieces of eight, so you will know the cost of this toxic system, so you will be prepared for the death coins of Hades, so you will remember that all food is tainted by his spell.[11]

---

[11] The Greeks put coins in the mouths of the dead so that they could give Charon, the boatman in the underworld, the "fare" to cross over the River Lethe (or sometimes the River Styx) into the land of the dead. Otherwise, without proper burial and the coin, you were left to stand on the shore. One of the more common side effects of chemo is a metallic taste in the mouth.

Soon, anxiety over the treatments that summer shrank my appetite, and then dried up the yen for food almost completely. Mostly I didn't like eating at all. There was a blockage at the top of my esophagus that everything had to climb over: vitamin pills, tea, filet mignon. Small bites worked best. But that was when something APPEALED to make me want to clamber over that omphalos at the top of my throat.

First principle and throughout—anything FRESH awakened the taste buds: sun-warmed tomatoes from somebody's garden; avocados soft to the touch; cilantro I could smell as I put it in the grocery bag. The freshest sushi in town, so I could fairly see the tuna leaping in the light—anything straight from the earth, the sea, the sky. If someone had served me a cloud, I would have buried my face in the pure whiteness and lapped the spun cottony feast.

So, when I would coax myself, Lilliputian amounts prevailed. I was, when dining out, the queen of doggy bags, for I would often only eat two mouthfuls before I could tolerate no more. And I couldn't bear for Ken to pay for a full meal. So the refrigerator got stocked with Styrofoam containers, hoping to be emptied.

Then I read a book about what to eat when you don't feel like eating, based on coaxing the finicky appetites of cancer patients. Color was the guide: orange for "change," which is food like sweet potatoes and apricots that seemed to appeal to these patients. Buddhist monks dress for transformation in those orange robes. We had all kinds of Buddhas in Ken's house, so I was reminded of the monks' mission, but I still couldn't eat orange food.

There were reproaches from the nurses when I went for treatment and they weighed me.

"Still losing, Carole? Why don't you have a chocolate ice cream sundae when you leave here?"

Shakyamuni striding

The one Buddha who might have shocked me into eating was the life-size statue of Shakyamuni—the Buddha of starvation—next to the door of the den. Youthful, and thinking he was on the path to enlightenment, Buddha deprived himself of sleep and food for many months. It turned out this didn't work, but Buddhists respect this stage of his journey and revere the emaciated god. I liked to pat his arm as I headed into the garden. In this carved wooden statue, the form showed sharp bones in his hands, feet, and especially his chest. His face was skeletal, with bony cheeks, and the head had a huge bump on the top. Ken said it was his "brain." He had eaten so little and meditated so much that his mind rose out of his skull. It was like a PhD in tumor form. Shakyamuni did not reproach me for losing weight; and although he was a little scary, I warmed to him. What I liked was not only his obvious "earned" intelligence but also that he was in motion: his cloak flipped out with his stride; his fierce, lined expression was determined and focused. He was walking away from denial, from starvation. He would ultimately find the middle road of true enlightenment.

And I would one day, I told myself, enjoy a stiff drink again.

Losing the taste for martinis: this was a great deprivation at first. When I tried to sip one two weeks after chemo started, it just didn't please the way it used to. Here it was: a mixture of vodka and vermouth, but it was as if my taste buds had been *re-virginated*; my mouth had become the mouth of a nun. At last, I thought grimly, a Carmelite. A mean side effect, a martini hit the tongue like a violation, not a Park Avenue luxury in a glass shaped like a wing in the hand. Oh, how I used to love that first stinging sip, trying not to spill and placing the long stem on the cocktail napkin just so, turning to the evening: Let's begin!

Nausea was like an unwanted lover stalking me everywhere. I was OK, and then I would see someone eating a big sandwich at work,

Another image of Shakyamuni

and suddenly there would be the big N out of the corner of my eye. At parties, I turned my back on the food table and asked the hostess for ginger tea, embarrassed for the request. I felt like the princess and the pea, with a change: all I could eat would be the pea. Once when I was quite young in the '70s, I went to a dinner party in the Village and the host served us on a dessert plate—TCP, a psychedelic drug. That was the portion size I longed for, if not the drug. One friend gave me marijuana with great enthusiasm, that I might finally join her in loving the weed. Although it was supposed to help the side effects of chemo, I found it made me sicker.

Pregnancy had also brought me, twice, nausea. But it was a different creature from the chemo type. It was, for me, isolated in the first trimester; nausea—one of the ways I knew I was pregnant. After that, getting sick, while certainly no fun, reminded me of the life within. But it was manageable; sometimes I could banish it with a cracker or a nap. Not so with chemo, which had the miasma more of a vicious kidnapper than a tap on the shoulder that a child is within.

Some comfort came when I knew, after the first pregnancy, that morning sickness would be replaced by that tugging heaviness at the root of me, then the distinct movement of my sons—those amazing bumps in my belly from their kicks in the ninth month. Nausea in pregnancy is lighter, more fleeting; at least it was for me. Chemo was a reminder not of life, but of toxins and fatality. As I gained weight with James and David and forgot about nausea as the gestation progressed, I lost weight on the battleground with cancer.

Then there was the old tradition of nausea in pregnancy that could mitigate the misery. Princess Kate of England apparently suffered dreadfully in her pregnancies (according to the newspaper accounts and her photographs). Adulation followed the sickened Kate.

Respect, even admiration, bathes the pregnant commoner; pity, the cancer patient. Or worse. Chemo's side effects for me always augured death. But not for all.

I remember the woman I met who told me that she was NEVER sick taking Taxol. "I ate steak and ice cream every day! My appetite flourished." Everyone responds differently to chemo!

I was far from steak eating, and fading away, it seemed. I caught glimpses of myself in store windows, mirrors—the model thinness had, by the second month of chemo, turned to Auschwitzian gauntness, with bone visible under the pale skin. Shakyamuni could have been my boyfriend, if I could just get rid of the passionate Nausea.

For months, a kind of seasickness had me in its grip, to the point that it changed my mood. Well-meaning friends would irritate me with their sympathy. I was much more comfortable with worry—it seemed to reflect reality. And my mother was a champ at worry. So I would call her to check up on my stepdad, who'd had a relapse from the colon cancer. I wanted to reassure her that I was managing.

"Oh, I had such a terrible dream about you. Your hair blew across my face and I saw your body in a car accident," she said immediately.

"Mom, why do you always have these awful dreams? I'm fine."

"Are you sure you've got somebody with you when you go to the doctor?"

"Yes. I have great friends who help so much."

"Are they good drivers?"

"Terrific. How's Paw Paw doing?"

"He keeps asking for another operation. The doctors say he's too weak. I don't know how I'm doing this. But God keeps me going."

"You're a saint, Mom … Truly."

"And, about operations. You shouldn't get your breast off until a year after chemotherapy. You told me you wanted it done quickly."

"Uh, Mom, let me get through these treatments until October. The oncologist says I should have the mastectomy in November, if I am strong enough."

"That's too soon!"

"Ma... please..."

Some days I would have a respite, at least in the gastric sense.

There is a hilarity in NOT being nauseated. People don't know, unless you have suffered this constant miasma of discomfort, what life looks like when your head is finally not in your stomach. When the eighth day of being sick dawned with a new feeling, "Hey, my stomach is calm," nothing could shake my good humor. Vacuum cleaner rolls over your toe that has just had the nail taken off. Not a problem. Verizon wireless bill is $355 for last month, after months of half that amount. "Well, I'll just have to change my plan." Ken misses out on yet another opportunity to talk to his doctor about a check-up colonoscopy, and I don't get mad: I just tell him sweetly that I will go with him next time. The world is divided into the stomachs on a rough sea and stomachs tucked in harbors; two kinds of people—the nauseated and the not.

Mostly, those first two months, it was hard to eat; hard to watch other people eat. I see the fat guy put a nonsugar substitute in his coffee. *How will that help?* I think. The huge plates at the Chinese buffet, food slopping over the edges, offend me. Stacking portions, a gross offense. How about the newspaper article about two guys who took the whole tray of scallops back to their table? The owner objected and they retorted, "It's a buffet." Gluttony, the disgusting sin.

Maybe that is why I love the Turkish plate that you cannot put food on in our dining room breakfront. The dish sits on a little stand for all to see, not to eat on. It is art because of the ceramicist's skill and the sultan's signature—the *tughra*, a great swoop of red standing

The tughra of Mehmed II (1432-1481) [12]

[12] Mehmed the Conqueror vanquished Constantinople (modern-day Istanbul) and put an end to the Byzantine Empire. Considered a hero in modern-day Turkey and parts of the wider Muslim world.

beside vertical towers—all rendered in ancient calligraphy. The 14th century bureaucrats did that so nobody could copy the script and make forgeries of the contract, gift, or tax code which the *tughra* certified. Only a few people could write like that. Similarly, today handwriting is almost a lost art, the joke of physicians. The pharmacist must take a special course in understanding their scrawl. Who writes notes anymore? If you get one, it is touching, old-fashioned, special.

This plate reminds me of the ceremonial, the royal, the identity of monarchs captured in a signature.

And I can stare at it.

That steadies the stomach. Once a colleague in the office contracted a brain fever. For months she was unable to talk, then slowly she began to recover. But for weeks afterward, she could not read: she could only look at pictures in magazines. Nausea does the same to me: I long to gaze, not analyze; to see, not understand; to look, not speak.

In those chemo days of nausea, it was so much better to sleep than to be awake.

And then, I dream of Shakyamuni. I take his arm, and like him, find a better way to Nirvana.

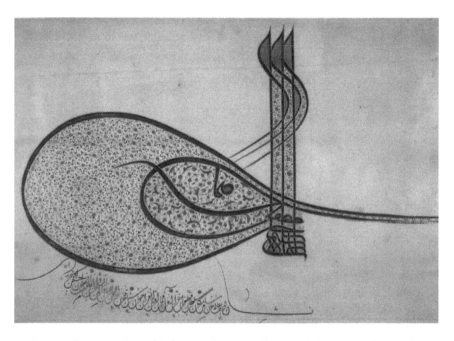

The most famous tughra of Suleiman the Magnificent (1494–1566). The words say "Suleiman, son of Selim Khan, ever victorious." [13]

---

[13] Neil MacGregor, *A History of the World in 100 Objects* (New York: Viking, 2011) 458.

SIDE EFFECTS

CHAPTER FOURTEEN
DREAMS

Open up your mind.
Let your fantasies unwind
In this darkness that you know you cannot fight:
The darkness of the music of the night.
~ Phantom of the Opera

It is Wednesday and I am at Michael's. In earlier days, I called him Dr. S, but now familiarity has led me to think and speak of him as "Michael," even though it is not my favorite name, being that of my ex-husband.

Now Michael was talking about the two kinds of "subjugation"—suppression of one's preferences and the kind where you suppress your emotions, especially anger. The first kind interested me because very often I don't push forward my opinions, like my girlfriends do.

"My friend Mary knows EXACTLY what she likes. Peter Pan collars, guys who give her jewelry right off the bat, and a LOT of gravy on the side in the restaurant, no argument from the waiter."

"Do you admire that?"

"Yes. It's comfortable when you are with someone who has clear and directly articulated opinions."

"Comfortable?" he says.

"Does that mean when I'm not definite that I'm not real? How about if the lack of opinion is just good nature?" I counter. "Or … maybe the opinion by an expert you have to accept," I mutter.

Suddenly I burst into tears and tell him about the diagnosis of the required mastectomy from one doctor.

Michael asks me if that is the only breast surgeon I have consulted about my cancer. "Perhaps another doctor will NOT recommend mastectomy," Michael says.

"It is too late," I say. "It must be done." I think of the Guanyin's flat chest, and mercy. This is September and the die has been cast. The oncologist says I must remove the breast if I do not want a recurrence.

"I am already shopping for reconstructive surgeons."

What I really wanted to talk about with Michael was not my decision-making about my treatment, or even my sometimes sudden outbursts of anger, which were surely subjugation flags. I wanted to talk about my imagination, my runaway, sure-of-itself, overconfident, make-it-up part of my psyche.

I wanted to tell him about my dreams

My dreams made me feel that my body was a battlefield with a civil war going on. Each night my imagination roiled with old historical images from my past. As if someone scraped the bottom of a barrel and brought up sludge, the images floated to the top and mingled with the present. The war image worked especially well then: the toxins were fighting the good and bad cells indiscriminately. The interlopers, the nonindigenous, were battling the ones who lived there, both the healthy and whatever of the cancer cells might be hanging around after the first lumpectomy. Medications also fought each other. Anti-diarrhea vs. nausea vs. homeopathic vs. over the counter—Zantac for heartburn, Benadryl for sleep vs. vitamin B for energy and nerves vs. Ginkgo biloba. No wonder I dreamed of taking the wrong pill. And, more, I was an internal Gettysburg, yearning to be home, to be unified, to be back with family, to be healed.

I'm exhausted in this stage of the chemo, but often I don't sleep. When I am at Ken's, the noises of this old renovated barn trigger my movie-making engine and my fears. Sometimes I hear squirrels in the walls. And every night I hear the house creak and click. Dozing, I conjure up elves with clipboards taking inventory. "Click" says the corner of the bedroom wall. "Upstairs hallway—check!" says the little man with the pointed green cap. Click, click. "Upstairs lab—check!" Click. "Man, woman, side by side in bed, check." Eventually, the elfin accounting makes me drowsy.

Some dreams were too spectacular. They come from fear about the mastectomy blended with my love of mythology, like the one of Penthesilea, beautiful queen of the Amazons, the fierce Greek battalions who cut off their right breasts in order to wield spears and shoot arrows skillfully in war. Achilles fell in love with Penthesilea just as he conquered her in combat. She died in his arms. Their romance, brief and consuming, graces ancient urns and haunts my restless sleep. Then there is Elizabeth I, and the Jacobean ladies who sometimes bared their breasts at court; and the nuns who had horrible fatal cankers under immaculate habits; they suffered death rather than compromise their modesty to healing arts. I dream of Nabby Adams Smith, daughter of the second president, John Adams, and her incomparable mother Abigail. She watched her daughter endure without anesthesia a mastectomy for breast cancer in 1813.

I dreamt a lot about the surgery. I was frightened that I wouldn't be strong enough to withstand such an assault. My mother kept harping on how it takes a long time before you are over chemo and that the effects take months to overcome. In nightmares, men in white coats slathered eels across my chest, and I woke up screaming.

But the doctors insisted that I have the breast off, and soon. Dr. Z said I was seeing too many reconstructive surgeons in trying to make up my mind whose technique I like best; whom do I trust; whom can I afford? These are the practical details that confused me.

But the most powerful force in my indecision was the fear of making the same mistake I had made in choosing Dr. N. This time I would not be seduced by a pretty face, a girlfriend vibe, a success story in fashion and demeanor. Cautious, thoughtful, I wanted to be sure I had the right surgeon this time.

In August, I go to Dr. A. His office is gorgeous, but I want to look at his patients. Are they attractive? What do their busts look like in clothes? There are so many orchids in the waiting room. Is this code for the beauty he will renew? And what does this orchid-laden service cost?

A very pretty nurse ushers me into the examining room and I disrobe.

Dr. A swoops into the room and looks at my chart briefly. He gets right to the point.

"How would you like THIS breast to look," he says, pointing to my GOOD breast.

"Huh? This is the deformed one," I say stupidly, pointing to the other.

"No. Look at this one. Do you want it higher, bigger? Do you want it to be shaped another way?"

"Well, I would like it higher, yes. Bigger, maybe; a little bigger."

"Then I will make it higher and bigger, and THEN I will make the other one," pointing to my nippleless breast, the one that looked like a ruined donut peach, "the same way."

Could it be possible? I thought.

"Yes. For $32,000."

The second surgeon, Dr. B, was even more of a pitch man.

As I sat there waiting for him, the flimsy paper jacket draped uselessly over my shoulders, I wondered why these surgeons didn't say something sympathetic when they saw the damaged breast. Surgeons, I was told when I worked in a hospital, are rough riders without bedside manners or empathy. The sharp instruments denude them of kindness, I guess; *cut, cut* instructs their training. My tears are irrelevant. "This is part of me," I want to scream, "and it was destroyed by negligence and a dirty operating room!" But the room blurs with my tears, as Dr. B enters, slightly fragrant in a dazzling white coat. He barely looks at the breast, and begins to speak immediately as if he has looked at my chart for some time.

"We don't have to do a mastectomy. We can go inside the wound and scrape out the tissue and use the outside skin for the new breast. We will use your tissue to create a new INSIDE and give you a tummy tuck; then lift the other breast to match this one."

Yikes! I thought. *I didn't ask for a fucking tummy tuck!*

"Will that still be considered a mastectomy so I don't have to have radiation?" I say with a bit of a lip tremble.

"Yes. And it will be better. You are a beautiful woman and you will look better than you do now after we are done," he says with oily reassurance.

"Oh, doctor. I don't like to look at it."

"When I am finished, you will be looking at it a lot."

"Really?"

"Carole, this morning I saw a woman who had a terrible cancer in her right breast and had the same operation I am proposing for you. She was crying when I came in, and I asked her what was the matter. She said, 'I can't believe how beautiful my breasts are.'"

"My partner, Dr. C and I, create breasts for women who can go topless."

I stopped at the desk as I was leaving and asked the price.

"That'll be around $35,000," said the secretary. "Insurance doesn't cover this level of mastery."

◆ ◆ ◆

During this time, I went to a party where an artist showed me an image of what one woman elected to do after a double mastectomy.

Remarkable, revolutionary! The boldness of the "patient" humbled me in my quest for a surgeon to remove one breast, not two, and restore part of me to a conventional shape. She chose to make herself into a captivating work of art, her chest a garden of brightness, a shout of distinct beauty all her own. I wished I had that valor! And that I knew such a gifted artist.

But at last, I took the well-trod path. After a final half-dozen consulting visits, I finally chose Dr. E, a down-to-earth breast surgeon from Roosevelt Hospital to do the mastectomy—because her waiting room was crowded with people who looked like me, a little somber, but their clothes fit; and, after my examination, she touched my shoulder gently and said, "Believe me, this is no big deal." Dr. E would also take my insurance. She would operate, side by side, with a guy who had a spectacular reputation: Dr. S on Park Avenue, a plastic surgeon who had performed the procedure I wanted many times: a TRAM flap[14], which would move part of my stomach up under the skin to create a new breast after

---

[14] TRAM stands for Transverse Rectus Abdominus Myocutaneous. The procedure requires a version of a tummy tuck in which tissue, fascia, blood vessels, and some muscle is moved up under the skin and below the ribs and rotated onto the chest to connect to the mastectomy wound area. Arteries and veins which lie along the breast bone are connected to the "TRAM free flap," the combined tissues, vessels and muscles from the abdominal area. Microvascular repair and connection is done with micro sutures and micro couplers under an operating microscope. The TRAM free flap is trimmed, tailored, and inset on the chest to create a breast mound. Above the mound and next to the armpit, the breast is anchored by a "pedicle," a knot which appears as a deep dimple.

Tattoo art from Margot Mifflin's Bodies of Subversion. [15]

[15] This tattoo process on the area where breasts have been removed is sensitive, even dangerous. Only a few tattoo artists are so skilled. This one was done by Tina Bafaro, and is celebrated in Margot Mifflin's *Bodies of Subversion*, 3rd edition, with full-color photographs. (New York: PowerHouse Books, 2013), 88. By permission of the author.

the mastectomy. Both procedures would occur at the same time, and although insurance would not cover all of Dr. S's work, I had hope that I could get New York State to pay for the kind of reconstruction I wanted. I thought I had a good case in quoting other physicians who said Dr. S was especially adept at this procedure, the TRAM flap.

The operations were scheduled for early November. I was still undergoing chemo in October, and oh, was I dreaming!

Over the course of two weeks, one particular dream emerged and played out over several nights. Fed by *BISBA*, an outrageous book on the shape of breasts blended with my experience at the various breast surgeons' offices, as well as an earlier shopping day with my girlfriends getting fitted for bras at Saks. This cocktail captured my brain in a hip-hop musical.

TITS, THE MUSICAL
ACT ONE

Backdrop: Images of naked breasts—drawings by Timothy Burr from his book, *BISBA*. [16]

---

[16] Timothy Burr, BISBA: *Baring the Breast's Intriguing Mysteries from its Influence (on man, mind and history) to its Inspection, Analysis, Identification, Rating and Interpretation, Plus—A uniquely valuable dictionary-commentary on a thousand ways to describe women* (Trenton, NJ: Hercules Publishing Co., 1965), pp 40–64, and throughout. Outrageous, thoroughly anti- or unfeminist, and engrossingly bizarre, this book, written with mind-numbing analysis, captured my imagination and my indignation. The notion that every woman's character "even to its most secret and private detail" is evident in the details of her breasts—this thesis is Burr's hobbyhorse, and he rides it into a fiery cataclysm of disgust heaped on him by all thinking women. The glossary of his made-up terms for the characteristics of women is especially hilarious. For me, the book and author became an irresistible object of satire, and actually helped me get over the revulsion of a breast changed by surgery. Burr's absurdity purged my fear and ultimately turned my anxiety into a circus dream.

ON SCREEN: 8 TYPES OF BREASTS: A, B, C, D, E, F, G, H.

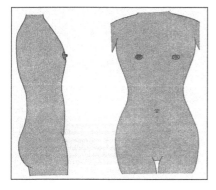

Type A: Arid, flattish, unshaped

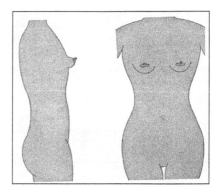

Type B: Baby, girlish, half-formed, ski-jump

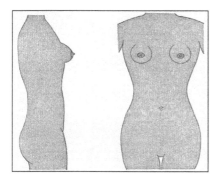

Type C: Cupped, bulbous, well-shaped

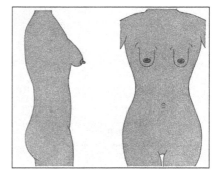

Type D: Dependent (droopy, saggy) but well-formed

Scene 1: Flashback: "Titty Camp" at Saks Fifth Avenue. Carole with two girlfriends before a wedding:

Salesgirls sing "How to properly measure for a bra"—they do a tape-measure dance around the girls—and then "How to put on a bra the correct way."

Head Saleswoman: Lean over and put your tits into the bra! And then tuck, tuck, tuck!

THEN IN COMES Doctor BISBABOOBIE! He is the self-proclaimed premier scholar on the shapes and sizes of women's breasts, and how their breasts REVEAL THEIR CHARACTERS. He is dressed in a coat made up of brassiere cups. Some are made of lace, others are padded. Some are black, pink, orange. Each is distinct and has a letter and number on it. He uses this "coat" of different bra cups to measure and categorize the breasts he comes in contact with. On his bald head is a rubber nipple which he rubs frequently when he is thinking. He carries a pointer.

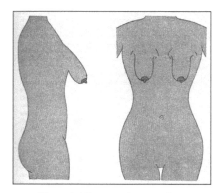

Type E: Elongated, appendage, sausage-like, well-molded

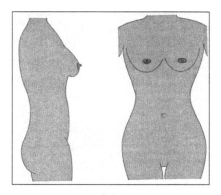

Type F: Fattish-looking, massive, widespread, matronly

Bisbaboobie: Hello! I am a gynecomammologist! Saks Fifth Avenue has asked me to give a short class on the breasts' intriguing mysteries. (Points to the drawings and photographs of sample breasts as he relates "the qualities of the breast as revealed in women's characters.")

CLASSES OF BREASTS AND CHARACTERISTICS
1. Capricious and annoying
2. Catty and disloyal
3. Irrational and panicky
4. Gullible and homageous
5. Wildly talkative and finds life difficult
6. Hard to understand and whorish
7. Poopoopous

8. Procrastinating and stubborn

9. Paganish and thrifty

10. Evaginatous and tiresome

11. Paradoxious and enervative

12. Dull companions and obsolescent

◆ ◆ ◆

Carole and girlfriends ask BISBABOOBIE questions:

Carole: What's poopoopous?

Bisbaboobie: She belittles others' problems, accomplishments. She is always going one better.

Carole: You mean, she "pooh-poohs" things?

Bisbaboobie: That's what I said.

Monica: What do small breasts mean?

Bisbaboobie: Intelligence.

Mary: Suppose a woman changes her breasts?

Bisbaboobie: Her character will be remodeled accordingly ... at least a little bit. She can also change her breasts by remolding her character!! I've seen it!

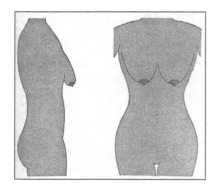 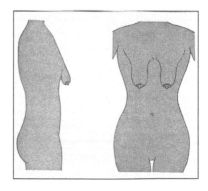

Type G: Galligaskins (floppy, plus-for knickers, breeches)   *Type H: Hanging, suspended, pendu-lous, irregular*

101

But now I must continue my search for the perfect A-plus Class 10 breast to complete my taxonomy. May I peek? (He goes over to the girlfriends to check out their breasts, but they run away.)

Carole: There's one more breast type. The picture doesn't have anything in it. It's called X.

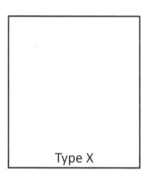

Type X

Dr. Bisbaboobie: That's EXtrinsic, surgically altered, falsely shaped. (He leaves.)

Carole: That will be me—type X. Oh God.

A dance number by the salesgirls and the gynecomammologist to the tune of "Tits and Ass" from *Chorus Line.* They dance offstage.

Scene 2: With friends around Carole. They sing in HIP-HOP:

Oh, you poor thing
Go to Sloan Kettering
Why don't you go to Canada and get Laetrile?
Don't eat meat or shellfish
Eat goji berries and never knish!
Meditate, don't fornicate; and don't be late
for Yoga!

ACT TWO

Scene 1: CHEMO Center, three women: Kathy, Lisa, and Carole, in Barcaloungers

Kathy sings: Finding the Vein (HIP-HOP)

Finding the vein/ finding the vein/ It's a real pain finding the vein
I'm going insane/ my arm is aflame/ oh, when will the IV be innnnn?
Gin is what I'm thinking of; that is a martini, but that's a long way off
I'm lifting instead my arm for the prick and hoping she'll stick it smoooooooth
And she's finding the vein, finding the vein.

Gina, the aide: Baggy pants, ex-cop T-shirt, short hair, tattoos, sings: WHADYANEED? (HIP-HOP)

Lollipops, Kleenex,
Gotta go pee?
I can unhook yuh
One two three!
How about a laugh?/ When the IV sticks?
I'm as good as Vegas with my schticks!
Cancer's a son of a gun; and chemo sucks
But for a few hours, I'm your bitch, baby
You're in luck!
Chorus: I'm your bitch, baby!
For a little while;
Make you happy; make you smile
Have a sucker; green or red
Might as well giggle, before you're dead
I'm your bitch, baby. Whatdoyaneed?
Without me, you'd never pee
Bitch Baby, Bitch Baby, nice as can be.

Scene 2: Cindy, the chemo nurse, sings to the men in the waiting room: "Sleeping with bald women" (a ballad to the tune of "Moonlight Becomes Her")

Sleeping with Bald Women:
You never would know
It could be a turn-on or maybe no.
Think of her as a cute little boy
Or a pal who's going through a tough phase,
And if that doesn't work, then get out your toys,
She prob-ab-ly doesn't want sex anyway.

ACT THREE

Scene 1

Carole goes from doctor to doctor, allowing their pitches for reconstruction.

A group of doctors in fugue, singing to her.

1st doctor: *I can get the bad stuff out and keep your titty there.*

2nd doctor: *Aw, take the whole thing off; live longer, many swear.*

3rd doctor: *Take it off, and for a new one, use your fat!*

4th doctor: *How about a double whammy—tummy tuck and cut the yucky breast—no worries after that.*

All: *I could get the cancer out and you will still look great!*
A little pain, a lot of dough, but hey, you never know.
There may not be many years before you're back
Because the monster has backtracked.
Yeah, backtracked, backtracked, backtracked.

They dance offstage.

Scene Two: ON SCREEN: The Park Avenue Office of Dr. M. S.

Carole in a waiting room, staring at the patients. *Do they have great busts? I wish she would put that magazine down so I could see. Oh, nice.* She looks up and smiles: "He's the ONE!"

Dr. S sings: "Uplift" (a hymn to the tune of "Jerusalem the Golden")
The Breast as Holy Object.
Woman's breast is a holy thing;
About it, I often sing.
I can take a tummy and turn it into a breast,
A place for your lover to nest;
A perfectly new and wonderful mound to replace the infected mess:
These are the miracles I do best.
All will admit who admire Uplift
I am the Sultan of Tits.

He escorts a smiling Carole off the stage.

THE END

SIDE EFFECTS

CHAPTER FIFTEEN
CAPE MAY

With the midway point of chemo behind me, and shopping for the right doctors to do the mastectomy and reconstruction complete, my tasks in August were 1) to get through the last medication in chemo, and 2) to persuade the insurance companies to pay for the reconstruction I wanted by the doctor I selected, the "Sultan of Tits," who was the star of my dream musical.

Thinking I was in the home stretch, I cheerily put out my arm for the first dosage of Taxol at what I was now calling familiarly the "chemo farm." The next day, Ken was going to take me to Cape May, New Jersey, for Labor Day weekend, and I was excited about driving down to the beach in a little silver sports car he had just leased called a "TT," a two-seater, fast and spiffy. I chatted away with the head nurse and tried not to notice the woman at the end of the row. This was Carla, in her 70s with a strained smile and a bandaged foot. Suffering with lung cancer that had metastasized, she was back for a second round of chemo. A second round— sounded like a death sentence to me. How could one bear to go through all this again?

But, as my mother used to say, "Life is sweet, no matter what," and I smiled wanly at Carla and read my magazine, pushing her vague prognosis that the nurse had muttered to me out of mind. Instead, I wanted to think about what I would wear that weekend.

I couldn't go in the ocean, but it would be fun to plan outfits for a couple of dinners out. On the next morning, I tucked myself next to Ken in the cradling, dove-gray leather seat. The trip was long, and I dozed through much of the Garden State Parkway, but I perked up at the Mission Inn, our destination—a reconstruction of a Mexican hacienda a few blocks from the water. Our room had wonderful frescoes and a spectacular shower with eight shower heads aimed at every body part. The owner/hostess was warm and hospitable, and the other four guests engaged our interest at breakfast. One woman actually had gone through chemo the year before, and I was heartened until she told me that she had no side effects to speak of and ate like a horse for most of the treatment. I was so envious, and humbled, I was glad when she left the next day, and I didn't have to speak to her again.

It was a sophisticated, easygoing atmosphere in a beautifully decorated pensione. But the second day, something felt wrong. I could barely walk the two blocks to the beach, and after I got there, I needed to go back almost immediately to use the gorgeous bathroom, and not for the shower.

Anything ingested, other than water, set off another cycle of nausea and diarrhea. I napped, then tried to get ready for dinner, determined not to spoil a precious holiday for Ken. A simple broth was manageable for me at a cozy adobe restaurant, but I was desperate to get back to sleep at the inn. The night was restless and disturbing, and the next morning Ken wanted—I could tell—to get me back home as soon as possible. He was, for one of the rare times, openly concerned. In the car, I could not lift my head, but I was aware of the speedometer hovering around 100 mph. I keenly felt I was slipping away, out of consciousness. There was no pain, but rather a kind of letting go—as if I were gently but firmly, like

Elizabeth Barrett Browning, being pulled by her hair into love. I knew, instead, without panic, but with a terrible assurance, that I was being pulled out of life.

I must have been babbling that when Ken told me he was taking me directly to the oncologist's office. "It's not the cancer, honey. It's the treatment doing this. I think it's the new medication."

He turned to look at me. "Hold on," he said.

The little silver sports car roared.

When I got to Dr. M's office an hour or so later (Ken had driven a three-hour trip in an hour and a half), I leaned against the doorjamb to the treatment room and told the nurses that I felt as if I were dying.

They immediately put me on an IV for dehydration and brought in a very serious Dr. M. Some sharp questions quickly uncovered a nearly fatal oversight. I was mistakenly taking my blood pressure medication while I was on the new drug, Taxol. The dangerous drop in blood pressure caused the overwhelming weakness and gastric upset. The oncologist team had not checked my daily regimen, and the chemical combination nearly killed me. A little longer in the TT and I would have lost consciousness, and perhaps inched toward a coma.

There were no recriminations this time.[17] Dr. T had many patients, for he was a popular oncologist. His office was always crowded with those waiting for treatment, examinations, and consultations. The episode revealed an understandable mistake in the context of so many medications, so many different combinations for many different patients. I also should have questioned the possible interac-

---

[17] Dr. T, my oncologist, along with Dr. N, the original breast surgeon who performed the lumpectomy, was involved in a lawsuit initiated by me at a later date, but Dr. T was not charged for the near fatal mistake of prescribing Taxol while I was taking a blood pressure medication. The case against Dr. N was never tried and was settled out of court in 2009.

tion of Taxol with my regular medications. But I was so trusting of
Dr. T and the protocol he had prescribed. Godlike, oncologists who
are also popular, even charismatic physicians, hold your life in their
hands. How could they make mistakes? Even if they do, it couldn't
be THAT awful, could it? (I repressed the memory of the E. coli
infection in the operating room and my first surgeon.)

We never mentioned the Taxol/Atenolol cocktail again during the last
months of treatment in that early autumn, but Dr. T did change the medication from Taxol to Taxotere, a milder form, and my last six weeks were
fairly uneventful. Death had, to use my mother's scary nightmare image,
brushed its hair across my face, or pulled it gently, to remind me not to get
too confident. But the Reaper, for the time being, had retreated.

I was determined to be at my physical best for the big operation
of the mastectomy and reconstruction scheduled a few weeks after
the last chemo, November 6. My friend, Dene, had been urging me
to boost my immune system by seeing a holistic doctor who could
prescribe herbs to somehow mitigate the chemistry deracinating my
normally strong constitution. My traditional oncologist refused to
let me take any supplement during the course of chemo, so it was
only a few days after the celebratory October 11 and the last day of
the Taxol that Dene could finally introduce me to a Dr. C, an inter-
nist who was also a herbalist and acupuncturist.

The office, however, was a shock. Dr. C's white coat was discon-
certingly dirty, and his waiting room was dim, shabby, and crowded.
All the couches had different slip covers on them, the TV was center
stage, and there was a grungy look to the front door. At a tiny desk
sat Dr. C's wife shuffling papers. But Dr. C, it turned out, was kindness itself, and exuded the sense of a gifted healer. He gave me special
mushrooms in capsule form (*Ganocelium* and *Reishi Gano*), instantly
diagnosed an infection in my chest, and told me to get back on fish

oil supplements. He also gave me Limu, a tonic which is supposed to help heal a host of illnesses. I felt on track for the surgery 26 days ahead. And whether it was the power of suggestion or the herbs, I was strong enough in a week to exercise and walk with more vigor.

I was preparing myself for a new life, but the financial implications were daunting.

Those last weeks of mild side effects had allowed me the strength and focus to fight with New York State about the cost of breast reconstruction after mastectomy. While New York protects the rights of women to charge their insurance companies for reconstruction after the 1998 federal law mandating reconstructive procedures, "The Women's Health and Cancer Rights Act of 1998," they do not allow "in-network GAP exceptions," meaning that they will not pay for your choice of surgeon to do the reconstruction. Because I had been injured by my first breast surgeon after a routine lumpectomy, I was intense about choosing a doctor who had an impeccable track record and significant experience doing this complex procedure, the TRAM flap. Writing letters to the insurance company, the Department of Health, and even my congresswoman demanded so much energy those weeks that I wept when I finally had to admit defeat.[18]

A mere two weeks before the surgery, I had to face the credit card bills for nearly $26,000, which would take me years to pay off.

---

[18] A conversation a few months ago with Sierra, the head nurse of the New York Breast Reconstruction Center in New York City, confirmed that, even after eight years, New York State will not give women the reconstruction they want and need after mastectomy. "They are not going to give you anything without a terrible fight," she said. "And women are facing mastectomies and don't have the time, resources, and strength to write, call, demand, threaten, and meet with administrators in Albany, insurance executives, and politicians who could help." She said she saw one or two women who, after months of advocacy and hiring lawyers to start legal action, finally won. But, at the end, nurse Sierra told me that what I went through, she sees every day.

SIDE EFFECTS

CHAPTER SIXTEEN
SONS

September 29, just two weeks to go. October 11 will be the last treatment, the last IV, the last day of exhaustion and copper mouth. I was upstairs at Ken's in the laundry room. Now totally bald—no romantic little fuzz on my naked scalp, my left arm in a sling because I had just blown a vein on that arm where the IVs relentlessly dove in. Never did they use the right arm on the side of the wounded breast. The nurses said this was the only way to avoid lymphedema on the vulnerable side. I saw lovely women who survived breast cancer but had to wear those awful athletic socks from the wrist to the armpit. Now, my left arm was threatening to rebel, and this week a gully appeared in my forearm—the long artery angry with use. Soon, if it continued, I would have to have the dreaded port in my upper chest—a permanent gash, the mark of Cain; chemo's angry mark saying, "I can't get IN."

That day I wore a sloppy sweater to hide the shape of both lopsided breasts, and pajama pants—the quickest costume to take a nap. And I needed naps. No makeup, of course. Why put mascara on no eyelashes? Why put foundation on drawn and sallow skin? I thought I looked a little like a patron at that intergalactic dive bar in *Star Wars*.

The sound of footfalls on the upstairs landing made me turn from the stationary sink where I was washing underwear. There, to my right at the end of the short hallway, stood my son James and then behind him, his brother David.

"Hi, Mom," they said, almost in chorus, grinning and loping toward me.

At first, I thought it was another side effect—a mirage of goodness, of health and manly beauty from another world, 3,000 miles away. The Taxotere medication had finally altered my perception beyond mere forgetfulness: the dreaded chemo brain! My sons lived in California. How could they be in front of me, here in New York?

But there they were, ages 28 and 25, so much taller—or had I shrunk?—than I remembered. They must be real! There was that thrilling aroma of young men. Helen Keller called the olfactory sense "the fallen angel," because when we began to walk upright, our senses of sight and sound distracted us from the rich information the nose can bring. The scent of young men was one of her favorite smells. Helen preferred the fragrance of males, especially the growing ones, to that of girls and their floral aura. Guys had the scent of rain and lightning.

Although both my sons called often, I hadn't seen James and David in many months, and it was sheer joy to feel their hugs, which hurt my fragile frame a little, and to breathe in their vigor—a torrent of muscle and health.

Ken had managed the surprise and the expense to bring them to New York. It was only for two days, but the visit lightened my heart and seemed to heal my arm. On the second day, tucked into a wicker chair on the porch, I watched them play catch on the big stretch of green in front of the house and the wetlands beyond. Lawn-deprived Los Angelinos, revisiting their Westchester childhood and the endless baseball and football fields I drove them to, they laughed as one or the other missed the catch and fell on the grass. After dinner, jetlagged, spent from play, they flopped down in the den to watch TV.

"A brother is like your shoulder," I used to quote them the African proverb about a man's major defense. And then, "Always be close." I left them there, and, like the years before, went into the kitchen for the well-worn ritual: the dishes, the prayers.

When I returned, they were asleep. James on the carpet, turned sideways toward David, his arms outstretched. On the sofa, David sprawled on his back, his right arm dangling off the couch as if he were reaching for something. They were posed in some imaginary football play, I thought, brothers and friends, catching the other's thrown ball, effortlessly.

James, David, and me in my study, October 2007

SIDE EFFECTS

CHAPTER SEVENTEEN
COURAGE I

My friend, Joan, took me to the opera to celebrate the end of chemo. She is a brilliant music teacher whose students appear everywhere I go with her. After 35 years of teaching inner-city kids how to love Chopin and Sondheim, Joan will sometimes meet one of them in Lincoln Center. I have been there with her to hear a voice from the end of an aisle before a symphony or concert say:

"Is that you, Mrs. Mallory?" They shift their coats in their seats to get a better look at her.

"Oh, Jimmy, yes! I recognize the smile. What are you doing here?"

"Why, it's James Lapine doing Mahler's *Ninth*! I'm here because of *you*, Mrs. Mallory," the middle-aged man grins at Joan, "in my 9th grade music class."

I was not an opera buff, but Joan took me because this was her favorite opera, and the tenor was Roberto Alagna. This was my introduction to the famous aria, "Nessun Dorma," sung by great tenors such as Luciano Pavarotti, Placido Domingo, and Jussi Björling, and so loved as to be used for years as the stirring anthem for the final game of the World Cup tournament, an enhancement to a number of movies, and an accompaniment to at least one Winter Olympics.

In *Turandot*, it is sung by the hero of the opera, Prince Calaf, who comes to a kingdom incognito and immediately falls in love with Princess Turandot, who is cold and imperious, but beautiful. Her many suitors must answer three riddles before she will consider marriage, and if they fail, they are beheaded.

Calaf manages to answer all three, but she is not impressed. He, besotted with Turandot, offers her another way out: she must guess his name by the following morning and then, if she does, she will be free and he will die. If she does not, she must marry him. So determined not to wed is the cruel Turandot that she orders her subjects to stay up all night to find out his name or THEY will be killed. Nessun Dorma, or "No One Sleeps," is sung in the penultimate moment in the opera when the prince keeps his night vigil, waiting for others to guess his name.

By this time in the opera, even before the aria, I was gripped by Puccini's rapturous poetry of worry. My mother was great at it, but here was a breathtaking mastery of putting anxiety to music, costume, and gorgeous song. I thought *I* had problems! But here was a guy so much in love that he was willing to gamble his life on someone not guessing his name.

It is in the middle of the night, and no one is sleeping—like me, many nights when I cried over losing a part of me that nursed my sons, that made me a woman. When I moil with troubling questions: Will I still be attractive to Ken? Is he with me because he feels sorry for me? How much will it hurt to make a new mound out of my stomach? Will I get stupid after the surgery because of the hours-long anesthesia destroying my brain cells? Will the cancer return? Oh my God, will it turn up in my colon? That's why I'm crapping so much. Where will I get enough credit cards to pay off twenty-six grand? Will I ever get my eyelashes back?

But Calaf is singing, with not a trace of worry, but with amazing confidence:

None shall sleep! None shall sleep!
Even you, O Princess,
In your cold bedroom,
Watch the stars

That tremble with love and with hope!

I am thinking: I also know about a love who seems cold or distant at times. Ken seems to love me, but is he watching the stars tonight and thinking of someone else I don't know … someone he sees on his European trips? My eyes sting.

Calaf sings:

But my secret is hidden within me;

None will know my name!

No, no! On your mouth

I will say it when the light shines!

When this ordeal is over, perhaps he will turn to me and politely say, "I don't like sick people, remember? You will always be sick because the cancer is within you. Goodbye."

And my kiss will dissolve

The silence that makes you mine!

If only my kiss will dissolve Ken's resistance, his silence about our future. If only I could get a really, really good breast restoration with big gorgeous tits to tempt him.

A chorus sings in the distance; these are the people of the kingdom who are truly worried:

No one will know his name,

And we will have to, alas, die, die!

Oh, I shouldn't be so selfish. I should be praying to live, to be healthy. Why do I want love too? I wish I had the sureness of Calaf!!

Calaf is certain of victory, that everything is going to be terrific in the morning.

He, or Puccini, makes me believe it! It's like the SECRET, just believing all the time that he might—no, WILL—make good things happen!! My heart leapt at the climax of the aria. Whose heart doesn't?

Vanish, O night!

Fade, you stars!
Fade, you stars!
At dawn, I will win!
I will win! I will win! Vincero, Vincero, Vincero!!

It is my brother's name, Vince! Oh God, I want to win. I want to live and be loved by the one I love!!! I want it ALL!

Indeed, the princess and her people do not guess that his name is LOVE.

He has won.

But Calaf goes a step further. He tells her he will die rather than make her marry him. He wants it all TOO.

I am crazy about this guy!

How can the princess resist him?

She can't!

They will wed, of course.

I so hope she will be good to Calaf! I want to see the wedding, buy them a gift, throw rice, flower petals, wish them well in person!

At the conclusion of the opera, the "Nessun Dorma" theme returns, as well it should, for Love has won all—her heart, our hearts. I grab my Kleenex and wipe away my eye makeup running down my cheeks. And hug Joan for my first *Turandot* rapture.

No wonder they played this aria at Pavarotti's funeral during the fly-past of the Italian Air Force. Yet, I am gratified most that the Federation of the Italian Music Industry certified "Nessun Dorma" gold.

The discovery of "Nessun Dorma" was perhaps more powerful than the aria itself. Art may not tell us how to live, but it may show us how we endure, and reveal that within us which is moving us to survive. There was an opera going on inside me before Joan's gift of *Turandot*, yet I didn't know the ending. "Nessun Dorma" gave it voice. God willing, I sang, before the biggest operation of my life: *Vincero!*

CHAPTER SEVENTEEN
COURAGE II

Instead of a hop, skip, and a jump, with rosy cheeks like
the little girls of England, the poor little things are leaning
heavily on a stick somewhat taller than themselves,
or carried on a man's back, or sitting sadly crying.
~ Alicia Little, Founder of the Natural Foot Society, England, 1885

The problem with me is that I read too much. Michael, my shrink, tells me that. He gets antsy when I want to share my dream, *TITS, the Musical;* but he really gets stressed when I talk about books. He just rolls his eyes. You can read TOO MUCH, he says, instead of listening to your inner voice. I love Michael, but God, he drives me nuts some weeks when I am sitting there in the shadows wanting to tell him about Shakespeare's definition of love in the sonnet: "Let me not to the marriage of true minds admit impediments." I study his desk and wonder to myself, *Where is his wife's photo, the kids' pictures?*

Maybe if I look at coffee-table books instead of poetry and great novels, my real identity will more easily emerge. I needed a big book of photographs, so I wandered into Ken's study. He handed me a picture book called *Splendid Slippers: A Thousand Years of an Erotic Tradition,* by Beverley Jackson,[19] about the barbarous Chinese tradition

---

[19] Berkeley, CA: Ten Speed Press, 1997. See p. 144 for the epigraph for this chapter, and throughout.

of breaking and binding women's feet so that they would resemble pointed lotus buds. This beautiful, colorful tome explored the gruesome practice in a beguiling way—by celebrating the remarkable creativity of the shoes created for the bound feet. Almost beguiling, for the cruelty could never be obliterated, even under the magnificent creations made to cover the horror.

I love to sew, especially hand-sewing. The rainbow hues, glorious design, and endless ornamentation of *Splendid Slippers* delighted me more than shots of the unadorned anatomy. I found it hard to look at the few pictures of the naked, mutilated feet. Perhaps I was taking comfort in the way the injury was clothed in beauty, the ingenuity of what I saw as a consolation for suffering. Little girls, at four or five years old—the earlier the better, so that the instep would not form— were subjected to this maiming and a subsequent life of pain, impaired mobility, and restriction. It fascinated me why this was done—to keep women down? To make them more desirable as creatures to be owned, protected, and decorated, like dolls? The reasons are respectfully offered by the author, but not for long. For me, the focus of the book is not so much historical as aesthetic and humane—I relished and was nourished by this notion so relevant to me: the extraordinary beauty of the slippers was generated by terrible suffering.

Where was the lesson here? I kept asking myself, when I opened the book to look at yet another exquisite bootie posed on a tiny shellacked throne, and graced by an orchid wand. Is this a version of shoe-mania, or as one store chain calls it—fittingly for a foot fetishist—shoe-gasm? One of the illustrations shows a come-hither Chinese prostitute standing next to what appears to be a curtained room with only a gorgeously clad foot peeking through the slit opening. We are to infer from the painting that the foot of the concubine we cannot see is resting on the shoulder of the client as they arrange themselves in

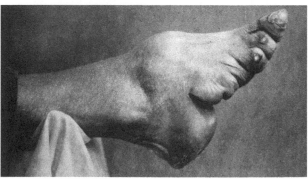

Shoe and bound foot, both from *Splendid Slippers*

bed. Tiny prettified feet make for big phallic lust, and lead to some specific sex positions. How will my manufactured "breast" manage this? There is no splendid slipper for such mutilation, although I suppose Victoria's Secret might offer some sultry options.

Still, the Chinese boots, three inches in length and fabulously sewn, talk to me about the way in which women have dramatically made the best of *what is*, copied nature, and then flung their imaginations into a spectacular new reality. Mincing through life, these Chinese mothers, sisters, concubines, and even rulers who appear in these pages don't often smile—why should they, when their feet probably hurt?—but their characters come through as quietly powerful. (Beverley Jackson notes that Chinese women often subtly ruled the roost in their families.)

Losing a breast is far less incapacitating than bound feet. I will take a deep truth from *Splendid Slippers* and find a way to create, in some metaphoric way, a magnificent sheath for my wound—and not just a black lace brassiere. Perhaps the account of my adventure with breast cancer—bathed in the most precise, most beautiful and lively words I can muster, like the embroidery of the slippers—will contain my pain, transform it with captivating design, and finally be useful and delightful to you, dear reader.

CHAPTER EIGHTEEN
DOLLS

Each time I wear lipstick, I am emboldened by the memory
of that day: the IV line in my arm, my surgical gown on with
my butt hanging out and my perfectly applied lipstick.
I swear I can still taste that hope.
~ Geralyn Lucas, *Why I Wore Lipstick to My Mastectomy*

If "Nessun Dorma" gave me a sound track for courage, and *Splendid Slippers* offered the first steps toward transcending the suffering I anticipated after the mastectomy, then a brief foray into doll collecting objectified the spoiling of the female form as toy. The language, values, and images brought me closer to the actual surgery ahead, steeling my nerves and ironically preparing me for a new body. The world of dolls rocketed me back to my childhood and opened another door to authenticity.

Innocent of this valence about dolls, but perhaps sensing my nerves for the event which was only days away, Ken called me to look at an Internet picture of a doll he was researching for an insurance claim. The price tag was $1,500. Ken said this was a collector's item—a Madame Alexander brand, which offers elaborate international costumes and wonderful workmanship.

The doll reminded me of my beautiful Aunt Ginny, who used to collect dolls with her friend, Ms. Toots. As a child I would stare at the dramatically lit closet with dozens of taffeta-clothed and bonneted models. They bored me. I thought it strange that my aunt and Ms. Toots, grown women, would take them up and sort of play with them, straightening their miniature underwear and smoothing their glossy fake hair, all the while crooning their admiration for this Scarlett O'Hara, this Mamie Eisenhower. Once I tried to hold a shepherdess doll with a staff and a tiny lamb in her arms, but Aunt Ginny gasped and pushed me away.

"Honey, your hands are dirty after that peanut-butter sandwich you had for lunch. Go wash your hands and then we'll see."

So I ran to the bathroom in Ms. Toots's kitchen and worked hard to get my hands clean, standing on tiptoe at the grown-up sink to lather my fingers. The towel fell down and I picked it up.

But when I came out, they had put the dolls away and were locking the cabinet with a tiny brass key that had a little figure of a mermaid on it.

"Next time, honey."

I knew then, at eight, that I was too messy to play with Scarlett O'Hara and blue-bonneted shepherdesses. Some toys you can't borrow, even for a minute, and even from a grown-up.

My own first doll was a stuffed dog with long ears, like a dachshund. Its "skin" was a soft, dirty tan plastic that, with wear, split around the stomach area, revealing the batting within. I tied the wound with a scarf to keep the guts from falling out, and I loved that doggie, often rolling up its ears in curlers when I played at "beauty shop," finally removing the pink spongy things so that the ears curved in a kind of page boy. Doggie fit under my four-year-old arm nicely, or could be kissed and hugged without offending me with sharp corners, like later dolls made of harder stuff. It was almost flesh and blood to my little self, or flesh and dull, lumpy, raw cotton. Doggie comforted me during many of Mommy's tantrums.

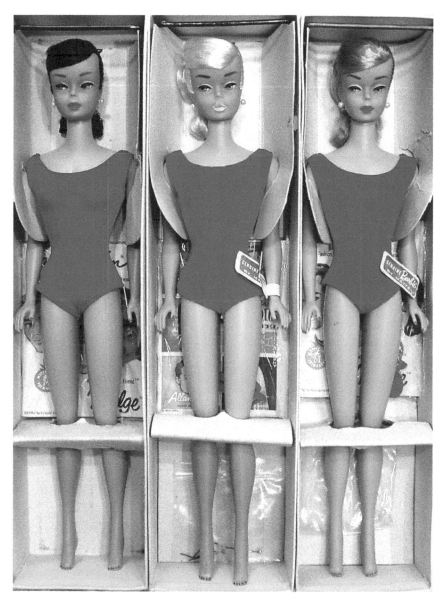

From Ken's research for a doll appraisal, 2013

But, more than half a century later, what I discovered through Ken was the value of certain dolls determined by their "not being played around with," or in doll collector parlance, NBPAW. Less poetically, "not removed from box," or NRFB. Dr. S would operate in a week or so, and I was preoccupied with "How will my body look afterward?" after I was played around with A LOT on the operating table.

Some of the most valuable dolls, I learned, are those still in boxes with the cellophane intact. No little girl opened this gift with delight, ripping the plastic covering; and later, slept with her doll when measles struck. No cough syrup on the front of her dolly dress. NBPAW brings more money, not joy. Some doll sellers write disclaimers about NBPAW and pooh-pooh this perfect condition on their websites, embracing, for their marketing punch, the approved sentiment of sweet little ones loving their dolls as they make up stories, and (aghast!) twist the limbs to fit their childish scenarios. But the praise heaped upon the new dolls implies that these sellers would be shocked to see how the hottest items—say the blue-skinned dolls inspired by the *Avatar* movie—are little-girl-handled at a tea party for *real* five-year-olds.

No doubt, the Madame Alexander dolls Ken researched were more valuable in their original boxes—tidily nestled, immovable, and pristine. One danger was the dreaded "green ears" from the cellophane staying too close to the plastic head. Doll death, or exile from sticky little fingers, or NBPAW can have its terrors too. And some distinctive features signal the real thing. Many of the Barbies before 1960, for example, "smelled like crayon" or had "chewies" on the feet, points of authentication. But for the most part, perfection is always the first choice. Buyers will dance with a little slip from the ideal: an eyebrow's slight blot, or a tiny hole in a doll sweater. In the end, dolls, like works of art, can make people fall in love with a darling fault.

I was alarmed, but somehow relieved when Ken turned to appraising the damaged dolls. The "never played around with" specimens depressed me—me of the wounded, uneven, and aging breasts. Here were, instead of glamorous toys, valuable objects diminished by fire or water. Sometimes the cleanup after the disaster worsened the dolls' appearance and reduced their value. Ken wrote in his report, "Many of the dolls have, in fact, lost their limbs and some their heads." Fading was noted "due to a combination of light and ozone exposure during deodorization." Ken took tender pictures of broken dolls, their costumes in disarray or gone completely. A bride doll was quite discombobulated, with her legs beside her and her shoes off. There were pictures of doll heads beside their trunks, giving a view of the engineering underneath: two hastily created vaginas. Their doll expressions never changed, while their doll bodies became pieces. With a shudder I left the tour of dolls in the doll morgue.

What I discovered through Ken's report and the doll websites disquieted me, but it would also make my psychiatrist smile. Bodily perfection had never been mine, but after November 6, at the Roosevelt Hospital, my own torso would indeed be less valuable, by some standards. Yet, looking at those blank faces, I recognized that my soul was surely closer to my battered but much loved doggie than to those plastic, blue-eyed, lace-riddled icons of my Aunt Ginny and Ms. Toots. Recalling those creepy, grown-up girlfriend sessions so long ago gave me the flash of a precious insight Michael would celebrate. Used, wounded, torn apart, and put back together, I would hold on to my childhood memory and, perhaps, in my sticky little fist, my true self, at last.

SIDE EFFECTS

CHAPTER NINETEEN
RHINO

I am the rhinoceros brought hither from dusky India
From the vestibule of light and the gateway of the day.
I boarded the fleet bound for the west, its bold sails undaunted
Daring new lands, to see a different sun.
~ Italian poem from the sixteenth century

The print of Albrecht Dürer's 1515 woodcut of a rhinoceros is so striking; indeed, it is one of the most famous images of the Renaissance. The creature itself was given to the king of Portugal, but he didn't know what to do with it; so he sent it to the pope on a ship. It never made it to Rome, for the boat was lost at sea. Very few people had actually seen the rhino, so Albrecht Dürer responded to the enormous demand for its appearance by creating a woodcut from a sketch. Printing was just coming into use, and Dürer was the master printer of his age. He made a fortune from the rhinoceros print, selling more than 4,000 copies in his lifetime.

It is still being printed today. I have even seen it on refrigerator magnets!

It is this big, powerful animal stuck in a frame that seems too small for it. It fairly bursts out of the picture. I have stared at that image many times because it amused me. What fascinated me was not that it IS a rhinoceros, but that is NOT a real one. Dürer never SAW a rhinoceros, only a drawing of one. He created this creature with his

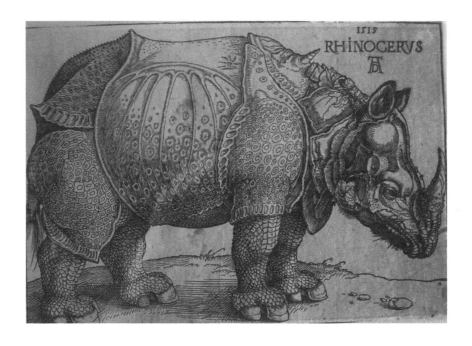

16th century woodcut, Albrecht Dürer

imagination, and it remained in the world's eye as rhinoceros-ness even after the actual biological creature was seen and known.

It has the color of a speckled tortoise and it is covered with thick scales. Like the elephant in size, this rhino is lower on its legs and seems indomitable. But something is not quite right if you have seen a real rhinoceros. The legs are scaled and the toes are splayed out. Most of all, the skin is not skin but armor. It stands out stiffly from the body in fancy rolls and flaps. A little extra horn on its neck is a surprise, and the creature is abnormally whiskery. It is also covered in small scales and swirls which manage to be both military and decorative.[20] This rhinoceros is ugly/gorgeous and monumental. Downright whimsical! Unicornesque!

In the days before I went into the hospital for the mastectomy/reconstruction, I stared at the rhinoceros with a burgeoning wish. I embraced this drawing as a talisman because it is a concoction of nature and art in the most wonderful combination—exactly what I hoped for after mastectomy and reconstruction. In a way, I said, "I AM the Rhinoceros—Sultan is my Dürer."

On the morning of the operation, I first saw Sultan in the curtained hospital cubicle.

He was dressed beautifully in an Armani suit and tie. I was naked and chilled. There were people talking loudly outside. Dr. Sultan was pleasant, almost thrumming with quiet energy, and focused; like the rhino. I thought, *Lively, fast and cunning*. He didn't look at my face while he drew on my torso with the black Sharpie pen. It tickled. Here was the artist's imagination in the surgeon who would remake my body into a new model with a more defined waist, a flat belly, and a larger, well-formed right breast. It would be me, but not quite

---

[20] MacGregor, *History of the World*, 482–83.

me. There would be a version of a signature, like the remarkable new horn of Dürer's imaginary creature. This would be the pedicle, that deep hole under my right arm where the newly fashioned mound would end, a final knot in the knitted bootie. In the last sculpting moments of the reconstruction—after the tummy tuck and the movement of skin and fascia and blood vessels from the stomach to the place where my old breast used to be—would appear this pedicle, the dimple; Zeus wetting his index finger and touching my armpit decisively, saying, "There! All done!"

"Nessun Dorma," *Splendid Slippers*, doll memories, and the story of the rhinoceros together gave me the kit I needed—a Swiss Army Knife of survival skills—on the day of the surgery. And hopeful emotions too: bravery, the promise of creativity after pain, respect for my own true self, and joy in the power of art in my world. And, with a prayer, also joy in the art in my surgeon—he who sketched his design on my body while standing in a beautiful suit. With all this, how could I not whisper, as they rolled me on the hospital gurney, "Vincero! Vincero! Vincero!"

CHAPTER TWENTY
RECOVERY

Don't Stop Thinking About Tomorrow
Don't stop, it'll soon be here
It'll be here, better than before,
Yesterday's gone, yesterday's gone.
~ Fleetwood Mac

After the surgery, at Roosevelt Hospital on 59th Street, I awoke feeling like Yentl of the movie, or Viola in *Shakespeare in Love*. Both Barbra Streisand and Gwyneth Paltrow flattened their breasts with long white strips of muslin so they could pretend to be boys. I had been *given* a breast, however. From a few inches below my collarbone to the top of my pubic bone, I was bandaged as tight as a drum. *Who would play me?* I thought groggily. Perhaps the drugs made me musical, for as I rolled into the recovery room on a gurney pushed by an orderly named Mel, I sang "A Foggy Day in London Town" to honor both the orderly and Mel Torme's great arrangement of that tune.

A Foggy Day in London town
Had me worried, had me down.
I viewed the morning with alarm:
The British Museum had lost its charm.

Recovery is a misnomer for this place. It is not a getting-well chamber; it is where the anesthesia wears off and reality banishes the blessed fog of the day.

The pain hit me like a Buick.

By the time I got to the 14th floor, I was glad I had paid the extra $1,400 out of my own pocket for the private nurse and the fancy private room. It could have been a suite at the Marriott, with the mahogany furniture and the nice lighting. But the dedicated care was the most important luxury. When I arrived, there she was: Traci, sitting in an upholstered chair where the two large windows made a corner. It was night, and I could see the twinkling lights of 10th Avenue below. Above her head was a tiny spotlight on her shining hair, and she was knitting. It could have been a Vermeer with his signature lighting coming from the left, where his only window was positioned in his studio. What a beautiful, if momentary, distraction!

Funny how rich surroundings cannot ease fear or dull agony. So, of course, I begged for drugs—Percocet, Valium, what have you got? And please, please remove the catheter. For the entire night, she ministered to me, bringing water, talking softly over my head as she rearranged the pillow, helping me shift my body to find a tiny sliver of more comfort, and mostly carefully doling out the pain medication I craved. She had taken care of TRAM flap patients many times and knew what to expect. But she did not expect the vaginal infection that I developed a few hours after midnight.

This distracted me from my wounded torso, yet I was miserable and determined to get the antibiotic I needed to ease the cystitis. Calls to the doctor and to the attending physician went unanswered, and when they finally DID respond, there was no doctor who would allow a new medication: it was too soon after the surgery. *The staff of the hospital is in the graveyard shift*, I muttered through gritted teeth. Finally, at 5 a.m., a compassionate intern brought me some relief in a dose of Monistat.

Johannes Vermeer, Officer and Laughing Girl (circa 1657), by permission of the Frick Gallery

Later, weeks after I left the hospital, this infection, probably contracted from the catheter, turned into a vicious staph germ called *C. difficile,*[21] a tenacious gastric bug frequently caught in hospitals. Only after my gastroenterologist prescribed Flagyl in dosages over several weeks did the infection gradually fade. So much for the protection offered by expensive luxuries on the 14th floor.

On the fourth day, Dr. Sultan unwrapped the bandages and showed me the new breast. The right one looked pretty wonderful even without a nipple, and with the swelling which curved around under my arm and into my back. It IS a better-shaped breast than the "real one." More surgery to make them balanced? Undoubtedly, but that's ahead.

---

[21] *Clostridium difficile, or C. difficile,* is a bacterium that causes diarrhea and sometimes colitis. It is a growing problem in health care facilities, killing approximately 29,000 people in the United States in 2011. http://www.mayoclinic.org/diseases-conditions/c-difficile/basics/definition/con-20029664.

CHAPTER TWENTY-ONE
CHRISTMAS

In the evening of Life, we will be judged on Love.
~ St. John of the Cross

After five days, Ken drove me home to Mount Vernon, an agonizing two-hour odyssey up the West Side Highway clogged with weekenders escaping the city. I put the passenger seat all the way down next to him and tried to sleep. I dreamed of one of my visitors, Sandy, my glamorous friend who loved to talk about her ailments, coming into my hospital room in a huge black cape. "It's official," she said. "I have two duodenal ulcers," and collapsed on my bed. Crazy dreams haunted me again, this time, I was convinced, brought on by the five hours of anesthesia. I felt as if I would never get rid of the drugs in my system and their attendant exhaustion.

So I craved sweet oblivion as if sleep were a medicine pouring into me, or hands stroking an ache. Shakespeare's "sleep that knits up the raveled sleeve of care" was knitting up my new body. "Nature's balm," the Bard called it, and for two weeks I drank that balm as if my life depended upon it.

Sending Ken home to the country, I groggily greeted my old friend Mary from Baltimore, who wanted to take care of me in my co-op. Generously, she stayed for nine days, serving me meals when I could stay awake to eat a little. She kept me out of the kitchen and answered the phone, later whispering reports on the calls. Her boredom stoked by my long naps, my friend began to reorganize closets and whole rooms, so that after Mary left I was searching for items months later. Her last day there, I awoke in the morning to see the dining room and living room covered with bottles and boxes. Mary had postponed her leaving to clear out my medicine cabinet. The next day I was still looking for the painkillers. Cursing her manic ordering and blessing her affectionate care at the same time, I kept rummaging for the pills, while I thanked God for Mary's loving gift at that crucial juncture.

By the first part of December, I was ready to be with Ken, and with most of the ordeal behind me, I wanted to decorate his home for Christmas and prepare for meeting his daughter Whitney for the first time, and introduce her to my family who were coming from California.

I was dressed in sweat pants and an old shirt, still in partial construction mode for the renovation of the upstairs Mexican bedroom. We had moved the furniture around in the living room to accommodate the Christmas tree, and I was a little tired. It was cocktail hour, and I fixed Ken a small scotch. My alimentary canal was still tender, so I put my seltzer water next to his drink before the fireplace. Suddenly, Ken asked me to sit down, as if he were impatient to tell me something. It was December 21. Ken gathered me in his arms on the couch and said, "I want you to be my wife." Not "Will you marry me," but proclaiming his desire to give me that ancient title—I almost wrote *wyfe*. There was no interrogatory, so instead of answering, I just cried my assent. (When there are no eyelashes, it hurts to cry.)

Then he pulled out of the cushions a box that held the most beautiful ring I ever saw and have ever seen to this day—an emerald-cut diamond with 40 trillions. Ken had designed it with his jeweler, Hector, in the summer—that summer of nausea and leg tumor, of metal mouth, diarrhea, and nightmares; of losing 28 pounds, of debridements, and fear. All my doubts about his love for me, my notions of another woman in his trips to Geneva, my worry about a man whose business was beauty itself partnered with me, me of the scarred torso, a breast made out of stomach, irritable bowel syndrome, very little body hair, and the seed of cancer always within me—all these doubts faded like shadows in sunlight. In that moment when he put the ring on my finger, I flashed back to the visit with the boys he had arranged, the presents he would bring me in the recovery rooms, and especially the question I had asked him many months before: "Doesn't it matter that I will lose a breast?" He didn't say anything; just shook his head, put his hand to his heart, and, with the other hand, softly tapped his temple.

◆ ◆ ◆

I am always happy at Christmas, but the Yuletide of 2007 shines above the others like the star of Bethlehem above tinseled trees.

First James arrived with his fiancée, Kari; then David; then my brother, sister-in-law, and niece. Then, David's girlfriend, Carla. Then Ken's daughter, Whitney, was here. And we were all together, celebrating the engagement, this new brilliant brother-in-law, step-father, husband for Carole—Carole who didn't die just yet, and look at her so luminous with joy. So we crushed the awful geography of separation in bear hugs and laughter. There was a huge birthday party for David in a city restaurant; a family gathering at Ken's National Arts Club; a special dinner at the Players Club, and Kari preparing a gourmet feast at what was soon to be "our" home, though the new possessive seemed immodest. Yet, I found no reluctance to show off my ring and talk about the wedding in May in Los Angeles. Yeah!

Then, in January, a trip to St. Martin in the Caribbean. On the neighboring island of Anguilla, Ken introduced me to a descendant of the Duke of Buckingham, Nik Douglas, a British art dealer. The two of them were full of funny collegial stories about Nik's books on Tantric sex, and art forgers in Amsterdam. I liked best watching Nik's still noble profile, backlit by the blue Caribbean sea, tell of his swashbuckling ancestors in the seventeenth century, how the first duke lent money to the doomed king and received great swaths of land, and how the successive kings took revenge.

My friend Mary joined us on St. Martin with her new boyfriend, Don, a cattle farmer. He looked like Ted Turner and had a big drawl. She told me he was good in bed, but that she was embarrassed by his passion for pigeon conferences and his four a.m. risings to take care of the cow herd. Ken and I watched fascinated as he told us how he inseminated the critters, demonstrating how he shoved the semen up the cow's ass, his forearm disappearing into the animal's body. Don taught us country lore: what breed of dog was good for a horse farm, the best way to dress a deer carcass, why certain pigeons cost so much. These conversations emerged from our nights out with Mary and Don in St. Martin. The double date: a long-looked-for pleasure after 25 years of single parenting. The double date: when it was good, a potpourri of shared fun, friendship, masked intimacy, gender comfort, and geometric electrical charges.

While the other three talked, the breezes kissing my buzz-cut hairdo reminded me of how my world had grown. From the royal intrigue of Nik's saga on Anguilla to Don's forearm up into the cow's innards.

Life had expanded beyond my sickbed, the blood tests, the healing wounds into a magical, faceted, colorful vision of the world—velvet doublets and cowboy hats and horses and English meadows all swirling around me, and at the center of the whirl was my darling, Ken. The sickbed had become the bed of lovers, and the centrifugal force, whirling the rest away from us. And there, as John Donne said to his lady, the opposite force brought everything to them, making a little room an "everywhere." Even the sun, now so old, could retire by simply condensing his duties to this bedroom, for here he could simply "warm the world":

> *... that's done in warming us.*
> *Shine here to us, and thou art everywhere;*
>
> *This bed thy centre is, these walls, thy sphere.*

Side Effects

CHAPTER TWENTY-TWO
WONDER

The kapala in our living room hijacks your attention from the books, carpets, and anthropomorphic statues. You don't know what it is at first, this strange piece mounted on a marble base and bathed in the light of the window. You look at it from behind and it seems to be a shiny sphere of ivory rimmed in silver, but if you move to the side, you recognize it as something more sinister. Come closer and you will hold it carefully, then turn it right side up.

It's a human skull burnished by many hours of hand buffing until the bone appears like polished metal. Indeed, the teeth are carved in silver. The whole object is a vessel called "an everlasting precious jewel" used for special ceremonies in Tibetan Buddhist monasteries. Only the skulls of very holy monks are chosen for this purpose. When the skeleton of a great monk is available, the other monks, said Ken, piss in the skull to see if it makes a special sound, the sound that this skull could become such a sacred cup.

The kapala, the head of the holiest monk, heavily hints that we are all perhaps on the way to a luxurious and jewel-like transformation in another life. But, in this world, the golden urine sings the truth of sainthood: that the human head is the only "cup of wonder," a chalice that holds the sovereign moments of life—precious memories, images of joy, vows, and blessings. For me, this cup of wonder cradles those transformations that bridge this world and the next, like a serious

Kapala, Tibetan sacred vessel, circa 1900

Kapala, side view

illness you recover from; like enduring through pain, even death's presence, with the help of beauty, art, and spirit, and—as I hold that cup today and drink deep—loving and being loved in return.

CHAPTER TWENTY-THREE
ANTIDOTE

*The primary mark of a good memoir is that it makes
you nostalgic for experiences you never had.*
~ Andrew Solomon[22]

When I was 17, I had a passionate affair with a black lesbian named Mae Bush. The romance happened in Provincetown, Massachusetts, where we worked together in a restaurant called The Plain and Fancy, owned by an aging gay couple, Patty and Vera. It was a popular, cheerful place, especially at breakfast, my shift. I found waitressing to be an exhilarating way to learn human nature (yikes! in the morning) while I made a little money for college. Mae was the short-order cook, and, as I put in my dupes for eggs and waffles, she, behind the steel shelf, backlit by steam and wielding the big black spatulas, slowly seduced me into a forbidden adventure about sex, race, and self.

Extraordinary and intense, the relationship was full of poetry, danger, and the exotic. I became a spy in my own house in Baltimore (my parents would have been shocked with the blackness and the homosexuality of such a friend), with secret phone calls and even

---

[22] Andrew Solomon, "His Own Case History," review of *On the Move*, by Oliver Sacks, *New York Times*, May 17, 2015, Sunday Book Review, 10.

one or two trips to New York City, where Mae and I arranged to rendezvous in a very dark apartment on the Lower East Side (part of the demimonde of dykes and femmes she would escape to after her job as a high school athletic coach in Boston). The door of that New York meeting place had a terrifying lock on the front door—a five-foot metal pole vertically connected to the floor; it slid in place with a sinister clamping sound. The women Mae knew were mysterious, in their leather and somber costumes, but when I drew near, their eyes were invariably soft. I was in a scary movie around them, but I was holding hands with a friend.

Most of the time, however, we were together at Cape Cod in the gay-friendly Provincetown ambience. Two summers passed. The relationship ended badly with my hurting Mae's feelings in a needlessly brutal way: my casual *farewell forever* as I rode off into the beach twilight on a Harley with a handsome six-foot fellow, a bespectacled Princeton sophomore named Dudley, the motorcycle dust hiding my blushing pleasure, as my new lover and I roared off. Decades later, I am still ashamed of that. For while the affair with Mae was difficult and fragmentary, she taught me two important lessons about myself: a) that I was definitely heterosexual, and b) that I had a certain talent to transform evil into good. Mae Bush called my gift "the Antidote."

It is the easiest way to explain my final resolution with breast cancer—the first surgeon's negligence, the complications of the infection, the multiple operations and debridements, the harsh effects of chemo, the mastectomy and reconstruction; and the legal case against the doctor and the hospital. Ultimately, the alkali that neutralized all these toxic experiences—the gift of Antidote—turned these into base gold: returning health, vindication in a court decision giving me a small annuity for life, the marriage proposal I had yearned for, and this extraordinary chapter I am living now—in my 70s—unfolding daily like a Hermes scarf in a Fifth Avenue window.

Are there side effects that linger? Memento mori of that year or so of surgery, chemicals, brushes with mortal pain? The chemo permanently aggravated my system so that I go to the toilet eight or nine times a day; my right toe looks like a serpent's head from the lost nail; and neuropathy in my left foot wakes me on winter nights. Lifting anything more than 10 pounds is impossible with the severed stomach muscles from the TRAM flap procedure, so I have little strength in my core; and that condition causes, along with age, intermittent back pain. And there are aesthetic effects as well. Dr. S did a great job in flattening my belly and giving me a new and, with the adjustment on the healthy breast, bigger, bust. But now I wish I had smaller breasts, as I did when I was younger. It is not as easy to buy clothes with a 38 double D, and fashion is more in love with the smaller-breasted woman. Rightfully so, to make up for some advantages of the fuller-breasted woman.

And, I am not symmetrical. The right side of my bust is a little lower, a somewhat different shape, and nippleless. When I wear a scoop neck or lower-cut dresses, you can see in photographs a valley, a shadow, between my clavicle and where my right breast ought to be, and the line of the blouse is always skewed because the right mound is heavier. You will catch me pulling the right side of my top down when people aren't looking. Sleeveless blouses are out, and some bathing suits, to avoid the view of the deep pedicle near my armpit. Sometimes the right breast complains—I think the ache means it's calling to its natural place, which is really my stomach, after all—for a transferred indigestion or putting on ounces when I overeat!

All these tiny complaints I welcome, as reminders of the biggest side effect of all—increased joy in living, appreciation for every day.

Cancer has made me do things instead of putting them off—the fruit of being frightened of cancer's return. The fear never goes away, but neither does the savoring.

When I see someone going through chemo, I run and get wigs, hats, treats, and encouragement. It is hard for me to keep my hands off these soldiers of toxic cures.

I believe more intently now in the spirit world. Coming close to death, and accepting that it might come, changed me deeply. That is the transmogrifying part of cancer, as Mark Nepo says. It is not a return to homeostasis. It is being broken and put together: you are riven like a tree by lightning so that the light can come through and shape you as another thing. It is the breaking of the cup's handle so that you must learn to drink by holding the water in your hand, or drink with "handle-less cups."[23]

How is it possible to treasure life more and fear death less?

I found one answer in a painting that hangs over Ken's desk.

I didn't "see" it for the longest time, yet it was always there when I called him to leave the computer and come to dinner, or when he shouted out to me to come check out a picture of a Russian chasuble encrusted with pearls and incredible embroidery going to the Museum of Natural History, or a wildly ornate Louis XIV credenza needing repair.

The painting that hangs there in plain sight is more than five feet high and three feet wide, easy to gaze at as I stood behind Ken giving him a lazy shoulder rub while we talked. It is by the famous 19th century Japanese artist, Hokusai (1760–1849). In it, two men in 19th century robes face you, one sitting and holding a book. He

---

[23] Mark Nepo, *Surviving Has Made Me Crazy: Poems* (Fort Lee, NJ: CavanKerry Press, 2007), xxiii.

is not reading, but rather contemplating, gazing straight ahead. The other figure, quite close behind him, stands grasping vertically—and fiercely—a tall halberd. For a long time, the masterly coloration of the painting distracted me from sorting out the content: rich browns, duns, earth colors—for the figures, clearly outside on the ground— are graced by white touches, of the book, for example, and a gorgeous red in the seated man's boots, belt, and even face!

What is this pair about? Is this some Eastern reversal on the muse and the artist? Is the guy with the spear pressing the seated scholar to do more research, to make better, cleaner prose, to complete the book? "Hurry up and finish the thing! I am tired of standing here." Ken is not around for me to ask, so I offer my own interpretation: Perhaps the guy with the spear is keeping the artist safe while he works (or thinks about working). I peer more closely: the guard seems to have crossed eyes, which give him a look of vagueness, even stupidity. I think he can't read or write as the seated gentleman surely can.

It strikes me! This picture is a joke by Hokusai, who was known for his eccentricity and ingenuity. (He was said to be so sloppy that in order not to tidy up his home, he moved 93 times.) The guard is a clown with a spear much too big for him. The scholar is in too much of a bad humor to create anything!

Later, Ken gives me the lowdown on the meaning of the guard's weird vision and the scholar's apoplectic face. The academic is red-faced because he is the god of literature, who was often associated in Japan with war, martial arts, and wealth. Ken tells me that the god of literature—Guang Ping—was able to read a full page of Confucius before going cross-eyed! Yet he was also quite fierce (perhaps *because* of the difficulty of reading Confucius?). His guard, in this parody, assumes the crossed eyes FOR the god. What a strange and amusing attribution of literature to the military and to anger. So different from my own lifelong gods of literature—those professors I loved in graduate school, who were often pale and placid, and certainly without conventional weaponry.

The painting is signed by Hokusai's chosen alternative name: *"Manji, by the Old Man still mad about painting."* Hokusai was 77 years old.

Such an intriguing artist! I must find out more! What I discovered in my research was not only a remarkably energetic craftsman well into his seventies and eighties, one who continued to learn, create, experiment, and teach, but also a brilliant and amusing imagist. And Michael would approve: Hokusai assumed 26 "art names" through the course of his life—authenticity in action. His work was so distinctive, he didn't have to worry about a selfhood dependent on labels.

Hokusai's chosen subjects were often literary. He was an illustrator and a student of Chinese as well as Japanese narrative. And he was also profoundly human in his detail: a smoked salmon with mice; a fisherman's wife dreaming; a smiling, humble woodsman who looks like an errant prince. I am thrilled by many of his works, but I love those of his old age: the famous Mount Fuji series of paintings, dazzling in their variety and ingenuity, speak to me about a volcano that oversees humanity with equanimity; and especially the "Tiger in the Rain" and "Tiger in a Snowstorm," both dated 1849, when their creator was in his 90th year. They are magnificent animals, the power visible in their frightening claws and enigmatic faces, one fighting the rain and the other smiling at the snowflakes. Here was an elusive, humorous, unpredictable, and incomparably gifted artist who knew his truth, and got better as he aged.[24]

---

[24] Richard Lane, Images from the Floating World: The Japanese Print (New York: Dorset Press, 1978), 169–70.

Hokusai, Guard and God of Literature, 1837-38

Hokusai thus offered me the answer to the question of how to treasure life more and fear death less, and a coda for the future—to be passionate, have confidence in your evolving craft, and to create!

Hokusai was a little older than I am today when he produced the image of Guang Ping and his assistant. This artist's philosophy shall now be mine, thanks to that wondrous and curious painting over Ken's desk. Here is what I discovered about Hokusai, in his own words.

From the age of five I have had a mania for sketching the forms of things. From about the age of fifty I produced a number of designs, yet of all I drew prior to the age of seventy there is truly nothing of any great note. At the age of seventy-two I finally apprehended something of the true quality of birds, animals, insects, fish and of the vital nature of grasses and trees. Therefore, at eighty I shall have made some progress, at ninety I shall have penetrated even further the deeper meaning of things, at one hundred I shall have become truly marvelous, and at one hundred and ten, each dot, each line shall surely possess a life of its own...

Hokusai died at 90 (89 by Western reckoning), peacefully and happily in his bed. But his vision of improvement and accomplishment shall live on in me. His code, valuing age for its marvelous, increasing artfulness, his lifelong learning, shall comfort and energize me in the years ahead. In my heart, I see my mentor, the magnificently authentic Hokusai, transcending death while he pursues, ever madly, the deeper meanings of things, when each creation of his hand will surely possess a life of its own.

CHAPTER TWENTY-FOUR
HOLLYWOOD

"What the American public always wants
is a tragedy with a happy ending."
~ William Dean Howells to Edith Wharton

On May 24, 2008, at 4 o'clock, at the entrance to the Little Brown Chapel in downtown Los Angeles, I waited with my sons standing behind me. Sunshine backlit this scene, lasting only a minute before I walked down the aisle to Ken. But it is a permanent artwork in my memory. A gifted jazz singer sang to me from the altar "Long Ago and Far Away," and I smiled with brimming joy at the little audience gathered. The words of the song came from a deep truth that seemed to be ours alone: "I had a dream one day/ and now that dream is here before me... Long the sky was overcast, but now that time is past/ you're here at last."

VINNIE'S TOAST, MAY 24, 2008

My brother's house sat atop a hill overlooking some of the most famous Hollywood studios. The reception tables were set up on his lovely veranda poised on the edge of the valley below, the valley of the dolls, the twinkling land of cinema dreams. My handsome brother stood up to give his wedding toast:

"Carole and Ken, all of Hollywood is at your feet today. There's Universal right there. I've worked for them. … Then there's Disney over there…. And then there's Warner Brothers right down there. … I have my complaints, my history of 55 movies with all of them. But Carole and Ken, you don't need Hollywood. You have your own beautiful love story, better than any Hollywood hack could conceive. Well, let's try. The story would go something like, 'Guy meets girl and thinks, *Wow, she can quote extensively from all the major Shakespeare plays even after two martinis.*' Girl gets sick and guy stays by her side, holds her hand, is there when she needs him. And for that, Ken, my family will be eternally grateful. What you did is what a real man does. Girl gets well and comes out of it looking BETTER than when she got sick. That's the power of love. Guy proposes, girl says yes, and all of Hollywood celebrates. So let me propose an old Armenian toast, which is appropriate because the largest Armenian church in the San Fernando Valley is right below us. (I've always had the ability to make any transition work.) Anyway, the old Armenian wedding toast is: 'May you live a long and happy life together … with your heads on the same pillow.'"

*Wedding photo, May 24, 2008: Whitney, Larrison, Ken, Carole, James and David
At the Little Brown Chapel, Los Angeles, California*

SIDE EFFECTS

EPILOGUE

October 2015

Today, the two-hundred-year-old silver maple tree a hundred feet from our front porch heralds fall in the acres of wetlands behind it. Its majesty is just beginning to turn yellow. Ken says October 14 is the peak day of leaf color in Rockland County, and that is only a few days away. By October 14, Ken and I will have gone to Atlanta to see our pregnant daughter-in-law and son before the trees turn glorious here. I look forward to both going there and coming back. Even or especially when coming back means facing my 72nd birthday on October 28. Whether I'm traveling or coming home, I am happy to be fully alive. I understand at last Shakespeare saying, "Ripeness is all." Aches and pains, the obits of my contemporaries or those younger still, cannot spoil these soft, sweet days of ripeness, the sense of harvest, of being ready for use, this time as a grandmother.

In this miraculous chapter, going and coming is equally pleasing. Oppositions leaven my daily bread. For example, I live in the country and I work and often play in the city. I love both places. In fact, the blend of the two makes a cocktail of happiness and health for me. Rural life emphasizes the pragmatic, an essential balance between the physical and the mental to survive. A little brain, a little brawn solve the problems. The mice that sometimes invade the house and which we must trap with peanut butter; the bitter winters, against which we pit the big-hearted furnace next to the kitchen door; the fireplace and wood-burning stoves we maintain for when the electricity fails; the flashlights in good order; the snow shovels at the ready for our cars so we can drive to buy food and supplies miles away.

Hard-nosed practicality, yes. And there are country smarts. The necessity of skills infuses our ways: carpentry, gardening, engineering for renovation; the know-how of shoring up the holes in the house to keep the hard rain or chipmunks out and mama birds from building their nests in the attic; the lore of urine bags next to the lilies to banish the deer. Watching on the porch in late summer for the teenage bears who might lope through the wetlands sixty yards from your feet; when driving, turning your wheel so you don't run over the torn rabbit body on the winding road you live on. Yes, the country has a sense of the tragic. The city, of the therapeutic. On Fifth Avenue across from the Empire State Building, where I work a couple of days a week, among the tourists bending their backs while aiming their cameras straight up, is a thrilling, unending action movie geared to show how things must be fixed to be better, higher, or tighter, in this huge nest of humanity. The urban world I visit excites and then exhausts me; and it is absolutely necessary for my life's fullness.

So I take the train back to the country to make my art like Hokusai, "madly." But I still need the ignition of the city—its dirty pavements and its rhythm to get me back to my real work, this.

No, it is not all soft *and* easy.

Mostly the city is where I learn, struggle to learn, the technology I need to write. Yesterday, in the busy Microsoft Store near 53rd Street, a young tech named Susan taught me how the cloud works, how I could use it to bring up this manuscript anywhere in the world where there was Internet. I found myself weeping spontaneously at the wonder of it, and that overflow of emotion briefly upset the passionate 20-year-old so in love with Microsoft products.

"I'm 72 and I'm overwhelmed. That's all," I blubbered, crushing my Kleenex and looking back at the screen of my tablet.

Perhaps, I feel that I won't have long to really figure out all these miracles of connection and communication. I sense these are not really MINE but my children and my grandchildren's tools.

But I keep trying. This morning, I used the cardboard virtual reality device which showed up at our door with *The New York Times*. You put your smartphone into this thing that looks like an old-fashioned view finder, and look through it to see 3D images of displaced children in Sudan and Syria living among bombed villages, boating among crocodiles, or picking cucumbers at 4 a.m. to support their families.

In this way of telling a story, the rubble is at your feet. You get dizzy in the wrecked houses looking down where there once was a ceiling at the destroyed apartment below. The children's faces are touchably near.

I cry at this too.

I see these inventions as if they are beautiful packages on the back of a truck moving away from me. I run, but cannot quite reach them.

In the 17th century, Lord Bacon once said that the magnanimous man must "live in contempt of peril, in contempt of profit, and in meriting the times in which he liveth." I must live in these times when peril and profit are kings, yet that is not so hard. I have braved danger and I have not lived for money. But the times in which I live can sometimes wear me down a little in my seventh decade. Still embracing magnanimity, I sometimes strain to learn new ways of using the computer, the Internet, pushing, sometimes with tears, the boundaries of my understanding. Brené Brown, in explaining the best way to fail, says that "there is a huge correlation between a capacity for discomfort and wholeheartedness."[25] So, I will hug my wholeheartedness, wince, and carry on.

Love is quieter and slower at this age. Yet Ken and I seem to have more energy than most of our peers. We travel every year to Chicago, to California, and St. Martin in the Caribbean, and we have been on the great Cunard ships, the Queen Mary and the Queen Elizabeth, to see firsthand and not for the first time London, Athens, Kusadasi, Rome, Dubrovnik, Ravenna, Venice. Our harvest time is golden.

I have my own curator, my own professor of culture whenever I discover another piece I love. At home, Ken is my own private docent to explain the art from every age and culture. But I have a secret joy in privately revisiting the things which took me through breast cancer into healing.

The Guanyin still sits serenely in my living room. Now I know why there are so many versions of this God of Compassion. He is everywhere in Asian art—and a welcome image of transgender beauty, mercy, and nobility. The Guanyin is one of the greatest prayers of humanity, rendered in loving detail and variation. Surely it must be a cliché of comparative religion studies that the figure of the Blessed Mother, her foot on the snake, is so similar. In my mind, anyway, I splice these two figures who gave me, as well as so many others, hope and comfort in suffering.

Every day, to shed a little light on the shadowed living room, I twist the switch of the bulb over the Mexican *escudo* and throw an appreciative glance at Juana at her desk. I read a book called *Relicarios* and marvel at the artistry of the *escudos*. Here I discover that sometimes, in orders where the nuns were totally cloistered, these were the

---

[25] Belinda Luscombe, "10 Questions with Brené Brown," *TIME*, September 10, 2015, http://time.com/4029029/10-questions-with-brene-brown/.

last images of their daughters the families would ever see.[26] I imagine my mother ranting in the church as I walk down the aisle to my "mystical marriage"—one that would shut the world away forever. The marriage that never happened, my brief childhood fantasy. The rhino etching guards my dressing room. How appropriate that the Dürer woodcut is in the room where I dress to reveal the surgeon's artistry. Dr. Sultan, my Dürer. The imaginary animal, me.

Hokusai still hovers above Ken's desk and makes me smile. Is the guard really me standing over Ken, or is the guard Ken over me? I channel the artist as I sit down to write.

The kapala stares upside down at the lawn and wetlands beyond. It will always be a reminder of the reverence for the holy ones, even in death, as well as the mind's grandeur; and the Lownds book stays safe in her leather-bound case next to the Korean seated Buddha. The dolls I see now are the ones in pictures of my aunt, who passed away a year ago. I may offer a softer version for my grandchild, if I have a girl, but I would rather let her choose her own dear companion; watch what her heart moves toward. When I pass the emaciated, striding Shakyamuni, I blush, for the weight I've gained in this, my happy chapter. I can see the spine of *Splendid Slippers* in Ken's working library, but I don't look at it anymore. I buy comfortable shoes for my size 10 feet, with increasingly lower heels as I move deeper into this decade. And "Nessun Dorma" I now hear only in Olympic events. The cry of "Victory" has faded like the laughter and passion of my younger self. As a notable interviewer has said, I am "no longer seeking those major exclamatory notes of pleasure. I want a life that this pleasure is contained within it."[27]

---

[26] Egan, *Relicarios*, 61.

[27] Susan Burton, from *All Things Considered* on PBS Radio, "How to Talk to Strangers," *New York Times Magazine*, October 25, 2015, 37.

The jade cup is gone, sold to a collector in Pennsylvania, but I still remember it vividly when I pass the *schatzkammer* in the den. There are other jade pieces, netsukes, and so on, in the cupboard. The empty spot where the cup once was reminds me of our visit to the exclusive Jade Center in Thailand. After the tour, the beautifully dressed curator came up to me and said gracefully, "You must have been beautiful once." It was the purest kind of Oriental compliment, its gentle insinuation that there was still left a little loveliness, a remnant of its sparkling history.

Last month we bought a young artist's oil painting of a young lady and an ironing board. It reminded me of the famous Picasso painting of the woman bent over her ironing, but this figure has her back to us as she reaches for the iron. She is dressed to go out, in a pretty skirt and red belt, her hair tidy, unlike Picasso's worn-out wielder of the iron. A very young artist glowed when we gave her the check. And recently we bought an Art Brut drawing by a gifted painter with Down's syndrome. His studio, where others on the autism spectrum work, is called Pure Vision. The artists there create magnificent works generated by a direct and passionate application of what they see in their heads. Their so-called "disability" grants them a ferocious and brilliant focus. The drawing of Obama we purchased from there is a folk piece that captures the president's power, optimism, humor, and innocence with breathtaking candor. Authenticity shimmers from the frame.

Authenticity. And what about my own quest? I think it was helped along by my mother's passing a few years ago. Michael said that often when the parents of inauthentic people die, those other-directed souls have a new lease on life. They discover who they are, truly. Perhaps that is so for me, but it comes with a surprising dimension: forgiveness. I realize in perspective how much my mother *did* give

Portrait of President Obama by Walter Mika (2015)

me. In the eulogy of her death in 2012, I told the little audience at the graveside about her raucous laughter—a bubbly current under life—her energy, her almost "nuclear sociability," and her way of teaching me to love music, especially the lyrics of the romantic songs of the '40s and '50s. My mother taught me how to "find the words."

And isn't that a writer's mantra?

Authenticity is a hunger we all have, but it is stronger as you grow older. I feel sorry for young people wed to Facebook, a process of making your life look as glamorous and fun as possible. But I have also heard the impatience of this generation with this constant wallpapering of reality. As one ages, the membrane between your social self and your inner one grows thinner. And, as Oliver Sacks says, the brush with death thins the separation even more. You recognize that there is not as much time as you thought for posturing or pretending.[28]

But I am not so sure that to be authentic is to be consistent. Learning is what I gained with my excessive education, a lifelong habit that, if done right, changes you. I am not what I was before cancer. I am not what I was last week when I discovered the magnificence of Frank Stella for the first time. If you stay the same, especially as you grow older, you atrophy. Growing and learning often have an ache at this age, but Hokusai handled it, burnishing his skills until there was hardly a gap between himself and the nature he drew, between the tiger on the page and the tiger in the cage. The real me is perhaps a dynamo, not a stasis.

Authenticity is also part and parcel of collecting and loving art, which Ken and I do. Ken is the official authenticator who is always looking for the "hand" of the artist when clients ask, "Is this a real Picasso?" I believe this is a parallel process to finding the self. As you

---

[28] Oliver Sacks, *A Leg to Stand On* (New York: Summit Books, 1984), 112–13.

ponder whether or not a drawing is by Keith Haring, you learn how brushstrokes, choices of color and pattern, proffer a signature; just as your likes and proclivities, your aversions and attractions are, as Yeats says, the singing masters of your soul. Listen, as my mother would say, to those words.

Making my own life a work of art seems to be the best resolution of the odyssey to my real self. It is still a creation in progress, but I also see it whole in moments of gratitude and peace.

In the meantime, this is what I know: divine imagination, intuition, and the perseverance of artists to make beautiful forms arrested me—the sick, anxious, distracted me. The meanings of the art objects I love took me far beyond what the original makers intended. Through beauty, "art cleans the world of our self-obsession."[29] What I saw and heard in the sculpture, paintings, and music here swept me away from illness and misery, and showed fulfillment by reminding me that this was also part of life, the part that redeems.

---

[29] Roger Scruton, "A Point of View: How do we know real art when we see it?" BBC Magazine, December 19, 2014, http://www.bbc.com/news/magazine-30495258.

LIST OF IMAGES

Unless otherwise indicated, we own and enjoy all the objects listed, as displayed in our home.

1. **Guanyin (page 8)**
    Late Chinese Dehua ware, meaning that the original was made in a mold. Circa 1900 or later. In this version, Guanyin has an attendant.

2. **Jade cup (page 24)**
    Imperial white jade archizing (in an earlier style) two-handled cup, probably Qian Qianlong. Circa 1795. Purchased by a Pittsburgh collector in 2013.

3. **Our Lady of Sorrows (page 34)**
    Sancta Mater Dolorosa. A sculpture in the Church of the Holy Cross, Salamanca, Spain. Thanks to my friend, Alexandra Coronel, for finding this source. There are other versions of the Mater Dolorosa with only one lance to her heart. I prefer the multiple swords as a model for the Stabby Mommy doll of my dreams

4. ***Escudo* and picture of Sor Juana Inés de la Cruz (page 38)**
    The *escudo* is dated 1783 on the front. The painting is on tin. The portrait of and commentary on Sor Juana is readily available as the first published feminist of the New World.

5. **Buddha (page 69)**

    Second century AD Gandharan (from Afghanistan). This piece stands next to the doorway of the master bedroom. Since I stumbled into it years ago, Ken has placed it in a less precarious position.

6. **The C. K. Lownds Book (page 77)**

    This singular artifact with stitched and glued flowers and plants was most likely handcrafted by Lownds between 1860 and 1896, with many events memorializing the frequent funerals spawned by the Civil War. A quintessential nineteenth-century preoccupation, grief was Lownds's province and art. In poetry, hers and those quoted by her, written in the flyleaves of the book, she painstakingly copied the 24 lines of the "Mother's Lament," as well as her own verse, about "the young, the fair, the loved ones sunk untimely in the grave."

7. **Shakyamuni 1, Shakyamuni 2 (page 81, 83)**

    Late 18th century, probably Chinese. The wooden statue, which is 60 inches high and quite lifelike, guards the door to the den. Another image we own is of a tiny statue, a few inches high, more cheerful of face, but with a gruesome gut.

8. **Ornamental Turkish plate with the tughra of Mehmed II (page 87)**

    We purchased this when we were in Turkey a few years ago, 13 by 13 inches. I've included the famous tughra of Suleiman the Magnificent (page 89) from the excellent *A History of the World in 100 Objects* (Viking, 2011). Author Neil MacGregor calls the tughra "a badge of state, a stamp of authority, and a work of the highest art" (458).

9. **Tattoo (page 97)**

Tattoo artist Tina Bafaro, widely known for her varied artwork. Photo by Bafaro.

"A woman getting a tattoo is the opposite of a woman undergoing cosmetic surgery: one carves into her skin her own idiosyncratic identity, the other erases all signs of the self in submission to a commercial identity."—Susan Faludi, author of *Backlash: The Undeclared War Against American Women* (Crown, 1991)

10. **Photograph of boys and me, October 2007 in my study (page 115)**

James is on the left, David on the right.

11. **A) Bound Chinese foot. B) Slipper (page 123)**

From Beverley Jackson, *Splendid Slippers: A Thousand Years of an Erotic Tradition* (Berkeley, CA: Ten Speed Press, 1997).

12. **Pictures of dolls from Ken's 2013 appraisal of a collection. (page 127)**

See also Margo Rana, *Collectibly Yours, Barbie 1980–1990: Identification and Price Guide* (Grantsville, MD: Hobby House Press, 1998); Cindy Sabulis, *Collector's Guide to Dolls of the 1960s and 1970s: Identification and Values* (Paducah, KY: Collector Books, 2000), and eBay's "Collectible Dolls Buying Guide," http:www.ebay.com/gds/Collectible-Dolls-Buying Guide-/10000000177628719/g.html.

13. **Rhinoceros (page 132)**

Albrecht Dürer, 1515. This print hanging in one of our guest rooms is without the Latin inscription which Dürer originally placed above the woodcut. With the definition of the animal, the print would be much more valuable. But the print became less popular with the Latin commentary; thus the rarity of the complete image today.

14. Johannes Vermeer, *Officer and Laughing Girl* (page 137)
Copyright the Frick Collection. By their expressed permission.

15. Kapala (page 146-47)
This genuine treasure of our household is hand-polished bone and silver, and it has a place of honor in our living room.

16. Hokusai (page 155)
Guard and God of Literature (we surmise), hangs above Ken's desk in his study.
Katsushika Hokusai (1760–1849) is best known as the author of the woodblock print series *Thirty-six Views of Mount Fuji*, which includes the world-renowned print, *The Great Wave off Kanagawa*.

17. Wedding Pix (page 159)
From left to right, Larrison and Whitney Linsner (Ken's daughters), Ken, Carole, James, and David Weaver (Carole's sons). May 24, 2008, The Little Brown Chapel, Los Angeles, CA.

18. *Obama* (page 167)
By Walter Mika. In 2015, we purchased this original portrait at a special exhibit called *Pure Vision* at Rockland Center for the Arts. The exhibit celebrated the work of mentally challenged artists, such as Walter, who create remarkable pieces, despite Down syndrome, schizophrenia, and other disabilities.

THE TIMELINE OF *SIDE EFFECTS*

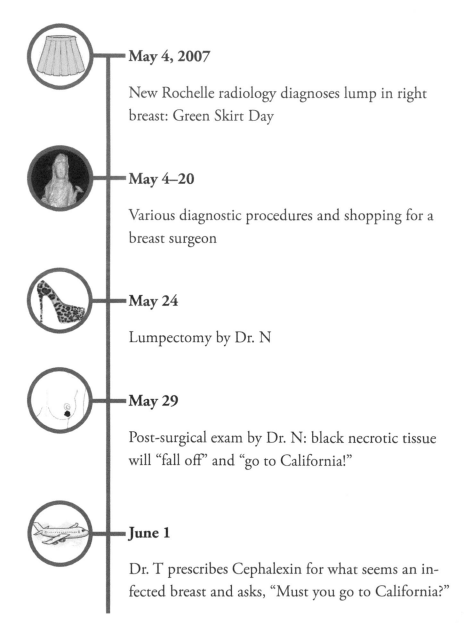

May 4, 2007

New Rochelle radiology diagnoses lump in right breast: Green Skirt Day

May 4–20

Various diagnostic procedures and shopping for a breast surgeon

May 24

Lumpectomy by Dr. N

May 29

Post-surgical exam by Dr. N: black necrotic tissue will "fall off" and "go to California!"

June 1

Dr. T prescribes Cephalexin for what seems an infected breast and asks, "Must you go to California?"

June 5

In Los Angeles, Carole keeps calling Dr. N, with no answer;

Dr. H, chief of breast surgery at a major LA hospital center, said he "never saw such an infection." He orders pathology report and drains in breast.

June 8

Back in New York, Dr. N aspirates infected breast, tosses out drains, and refuses to call Dr. H.

June 11

Dr. Z gets pathology report which indicates *E. coli*; recommends hospitalization

June 12

Carole goes to New Rochelle emergency room; fires Dr. N; looks for new surgeon

June 12–21

Hospitalization for E. coli infection, debridements, and other surgical procedures

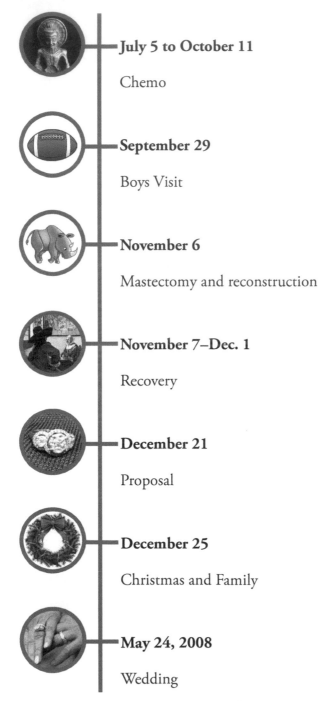

July 5 to October 11

Chemo

September 29

Boys Visit

November 6

Mastectomy and reconstruction

November 7–Dec. 1

Recovery

December 21

Proposal

December 25

Christmas and Family

May 24, 2008

Wedding

LIST OF RESOURCES

What I used for Inspiration, Comfort, Illumination,
Validation, Humor, Distraction from Nausea,
and Temporary Assurance of Sanity

American Cancer Society. Cancer Treatment & Survivorship Facts and Figures 2014–2015. http://www.cancer.org/acs/groups/content/@research/documents/document/acspc-042801.pdf.

American Music Therapy Association (AMTA), Senate Hearing 25th Anniversary Report, July 29, 2016, Courtesy of Joan Winer Brown, http://www.musictherapy.org/senate_hearing_25th_anniversary/.

Burr, Timothy. *BISBA: Baring the Breast's Intriguing Mysteries from its Influence (on man, mind, and history) to its Inspection, Analysis, Identification, Rating and Interpretation. Plus—A uniquely valuable dictionary-commentary on a thousand ways to describe women.* Trenton, NJ: Hercules Publishing Company, 1965.

Burton, Susan. "Terry Gross and the Art of Opening Up." *The New York Times Magazine*, October 21, 2015. http://www.nytimes.com/2015/10/25/magazine/terry-gross-and-the-art-of-opening-up.html?_r=0.

Calza, Gian Carlo, and John T. Carpenter, eds. *Hokusai Paintings: Selected Essays.* Venice, Italy: The International Hokusai Research Centre, University of Venice, 1994.

Cameron, Julia. *The Artist's Way: A Spiritual Path to Higher Creativity.* New York: Putnam/Penguin, 1992; and many *Artist's Way Morning Pages Journals*, 1992 to 2003.

Diaz, Junot. *The Brief Wondrous Life of Oscar Wao.* New York: Riverhead Books, 2007 (especially for footnote manner).

Dickinson, Emily. *The Complete Poems of Emily Dickinson*, edited by Thomas H. Johnson. Boston: Little, Brown and Company, 1955.

Drescher, Fran. *Cancer Schmancer.* New York: Grand Central Publishing, 2003.

Egan, Martha. *Relicarios: Devotional Miniatures from the Americas.* Santa Fe: Museum of New Mexico Press, 1993.

Institute for Music and Neurologic Function, music therapy at Beth Abraham, as reported by Joan Winer Brown.

Jackson, Beverley. *Splendid Slippers: A Thousand Years of an Erotic Tradition.* Berkeley, CA: Ten Speed Press, 1997.

Leonard, Elizabeth. "Jackie Collins: Her Final Interview." *People* Magazine, October 2015, 65–69.

Lucas, Geralyn. *Why I Wore Lipstick to My Mastectomy.* New York: St. Martin's Griffin, 2004.

Lunden, Joan, and Laura Morton. *Had I Known: A Memoir of Survival.* New York: Harper, 2015.

MacGregor, Neil. *A History of the World in 100 Objects.* New York: Viking, 2011.

Mifflin, Margot. *Bodies of Subversion: A Secret History of Women and Tattoo, 3rd edition.* New York: PowerHouse Books, 2013, 88.

Nepo, Mark. *Surviving Has Made Me Crazy: Poems.* Fort Lee, NJ: CavanKerry Press, 2007.

———. *The Book of Awakening: Having the Life You Want by Being Present to the Life You Have.* San Francisco, CA: Conari Press, 2000; and 2010 edition (Oprah's favorite things).

O'Connor, Siobhan. "Why Doctors Are Rethinking Breast-Cancer Treatment." *Time* Magazine, October 1, 2015. http://time.com/4057310/breast-cancer-overtreatment/.

Sacks, Oliver. *A Leg to Stand On.* New York: Summit Books, 1984.

———. *Musicophilia: Tales of Music and the Brain.* New York: Knopf, 2007.

Salerno, Heather. "Paying It Forward: Local Breast Cancer Survivors Help Inspire Others." *The Journal News,* October 4, 2015. 12-page supplement.

Scruton, Roger. "A Point of View: How do we know real art when we see it?" BBC News Magazine, 19 December 2014. http://www.bbc.com/news/magazine-30495258.

Solomon, Andrew. *Far From the Tree: Parents, Children, and the Search for Identity.* New York: Scribner, 2012.

Stancarone, Dr. Michael. "Other-Directedness." 2007 handout.

Tagliaferri, Mary, Isaac Cohen, and Debu Tripathy. *Breast Cancer: Beyond Convention: The World's Foremost Authorities on Complementary and Alternative Medicine Offer Advice on Healing.* New York: Atria Books, 2002.

Wardropper, Ian. *The Frick Collection. Director's Choice.* London: Scala Arts & Heritage Publishers, 2015 (especially Johannes Vermeer, 1632 to 1675).

ACKNOWLEDGMENTS

This book would not have been born without the Piermont Writers Group (PWG) of 2015, with best-selling author Jeanine Cummins as the coach. I am grateful first to Edith Knoblick, neighbor, visionary, and talent, who convinced me that occasional discussions of my notes over scotch on the rocks was no substitute for a serious writing seminar. So I joined PWG, where weekly increments presented to Jeanine and a small cohort of gifted colleagues helped me hammer out a first draft. Beryl Meyer, my first fan, Lisa Coughlin, Anne Miller, Virginia Sanchez, and the inestimable Edith listened with wild intensity, squandered their insights and suggestions, and with furious check marks they applauded sentences and phrases they loved. Beginning each weekly 3-hour-plus session with dread and ending it with tender confidence and exhaustion, we all cycled our projects through the year. At the end, Jeanine's agreeing to edit my final draft was essential. She is a remarkable teacher, editor, and friend to all new writers. Bless her, and that little cadre of writing pals that got me through.

My brother, Vince McKewin, experienced screenwriter of more than 50 feature films, read the completed work and gave me wonderful advice and support. Sandy Coronel, an old friend from graduate school at the University of Maryland, read and reviewed the manuscript and found an important picture of the Madonna of Sorrows. Thanks also to Mynetta McCutcheon, my former assistant at the College of New Rochelle, for her heartfelt reading of the manuscript, and, since she was there for it all, her personal validation of the events.

My loyal and loving friend of 50 years, Mary Sturm, who took me through postoperative healing by watching over me in my home, needs to be saluted for her ongoing devotion; and my other closest friend since the 1990s, Diane Dudzinski, sustained me through not only the illness, as is limned in the narrative, but also through many months of shaping the writing project. Her husband, Don, offered me valued creative design advice, as well as warm and knowing wisdom gained through his own cancer ordeal.

Some of us have jobs where we merely work; others have jobs which bring out our talents and our calling in life. My part-time work at National Medical Fellowships, which for 70 years has raised money for minorities going to medical school, has a mission which always inspires me, and it has also allowed me the flexibility as a senior consultant in fund-raising to take the time to write my story. My thanks to Dr. Esther Dyer, president, and her team, especially Joan Winer Brown, a gifted writer in her own stead, for her helpful advice and insight into the work of Oliver Sacks.

Warmest gratitude to Sheila Pearl for introducing me to a perfect publishing partner in Bethany Kelly, and providing me with the initial spark to move ahead with self-publishing. Sheila is also a role model as a dynamic speaker, writer, and leader for those of us who grew up in the sixties. It is a privilege to call her my friend.

To Dr. Michael Stancarone, my therapist during the toughest part of the story. His willingness to speak to me years later and reprise the major themes of his philosophy, especially about authenticity, only reinforced the importance of his guidance in my healing, and established a vein of gold in the unfolding narrative.

Dijon Parker helped me with important technological issues with graphics and the integrity of the manuscript. Her good humor with my lack of computer savvy and her skills saved *Side Effects* from certain digital disaster. Thank you!

For her introducing me to tattooed ladies, and her finesse with my final title, Natasha Rabin must be saluted and hugged!

Marianne Carroll and Carmen Brown, my spiritual guides through astrological analysis and ancient posture ceremonies, were restorative agents for the writer's need for magic to stroke and uplift the soul.

Joy Herald through two interviews provided incisive criticism and opened up the vista of a commercial publishing venture. I thank her for her honesty, expertise, and kindness.

To my longtime friend, Joan Mallory, a talented music professor, for bravely representing the lyrics to *Tits, the Musical.* With her considerable contacts and influence she found Seth Allen, a composer who agreed to set my words to music as I had hoped (or rather dreamed)—a blend of hip-hop, traditional, hymnal, and other genres, all at her cost. Thank you, Seth! And Joan has been an ongoing personal and artistic treasure in my life for many years; for example, I love her for introducing me to the joys of opera.

Bethany Kelly, my publishing partner, has been a fortress of confidence, serenity, and glorious effectiveness toward completion of the work. Thank you with all my heart.

To the women who wrote memoirs about surviving breast cancer—in particular Fran Drescher, Geralyn Lucas, and Joan Lunden, whose stories moved me and spurred me to write my own—I am grateful. If anything gives me stature in this memoir, it is because I stand on your shoulders!

To my good doctors, those who saw me through unexpected hospital infections, chemo, terrible side effects, intricate and major surgery, I bow my head in gratitude for your expertise and compassion. Taking care of cancer patients is a heroic and demanding task. I could not have written this book without your knowledge and grace.

For her generous affection and industry in helping me with portions of the ancillary sections of the manuscript, I am so thankful for the friendship of Victorine Froehlich. In the final stages, when my energy flagged, she brought a vigorous focus and bracing cheer to the finish line.

James and David, my dearest sons, thank you for always believing in me, for the many phone calls and deep concern and attention, without which I could not have found the strength and peace to revisit a very difficult period in composing the book. I am so very proud of your loving ways even from another coast, of the superb wives you have chosen, and of your families.

While the chief dedicatee of *Side Effects* is Ken, I need to thank him once more for the gift of beautiful, beguiling objects set in the home he has given me—a stage of gentle wetlands and passionate birdsong, for loving me when I was at the nadir of my health, for his contagious expectation that I would heal and revive, and (if the book hasn't told the world already) for our partnership, late in our seasons, of a happy, deeply satisfying life together. So it needs to be said again: Your brilliance and love have made this creation possible.

ABOUT THE AUTHOR

D r. Carole Weaver, teacher, business developer, and professional writer, has sculpted her life with three skills: college teaching, fund-raising, and single parenting. All have in common the power of language to make good things happen, often in the midst of daunting challenges.

A proud Baltimorean, she was the first in her family of steamfitters and very little schooling to graduate from college, then earn a master's and doctoral degree from the University of Maryland. In between graduate degrees, poor, but adventurous and deeply bookish, she accepted an invitation to teach for the university in their college extension division serving American troops in Germany and England. For four years, her students were Air Force, Army, and Navy personnel, and those who served them on military bases in the European theatre. Rousing exhausted enlisted men and women for 7 p.m. classes after a full day of work, Carole mastered the artful blend of entertainment and enlightenment, cultivating theatre skills that would serve her well in persuasion for the marketplace (as well as a stint in her 60s in community theatre as Elaine in *Company* and Fraulein Schneider in *Cabaret*. What fun!).

Returning home in the late 1970s, she became part of the English faculties at the University of Delaware, St. Francis College, and Iona College in New York, where she married in 1979 and gave birth to her two sons.

The adventure continued with divorce and becoming a single parent of a two-month-old and a three-and-a-half-year-old, David and James. Prompted by financial needs, she morphed into a grant writer and then a successful fund-raiser. Over the next two decades, Carole raised over $50 million for Iona College, Mount Vernon Hospital, Sound Shore Medical, the New York College for Wholistic Health, the College of New Rochelle, and National Medical Fellowships. She has raised money for libraries, health centers, science education programs, award-winning lecture series, endowments, planned giving programs, physician education and development systems, scholarships, and many faculty projects. In addition, she found her favorite role to be a trainer and advisor to start-up operations in the nonprofit world. That function appeals to her as a teacher and builder of institutions.

Carole has published academic essays on Shakespeare, especially pioneering feminist criticism; for example, "Shakespeare Liberata" in the journal *Mosaic* (1977) and "Counsels of Gall and Grace" in *The Woman's Part: Feminist Criticism of Shakespeare* (Univ. of Illinois Press, 1980). Other literary critical works include "Tasting Stars: The Tales of Rabbi Nachman in Anne Roiphe's *Lovingkindness*" in *Mother Puzzles* (Greenwood Press, 1989). She has published profiles of donors and philanthropists (Jean Little and Peggy McConnell) in college magazines, and has been engaged as a speaker at various professional venues; she was the convocation speaker for the graduation of the nursing class of 2003 at the College of New Rochelle. She has presented at fund-raising conferences and associations, such as the National Case Conference in 2006 ("Planting the Seeds of Philanthropy"), and she gave the Association of Development Officers' keynote ("Karaoke, Wheelchairs, and the Harvest of Suffering: the End of Year Gift") in 2009. Since 2010, she has been developing a TV series, *Fair Warning* (about the world of art crime), with partners Froyland and Birnbaum.

The narrative of *Side* Effects brings us up to date with her family life in New York for the past eight years. She lives with her husband, Ken, in Rockland County, NY in a home, which is part museum, part library. Their four children, two boys and Ken's two girls, all in their 30s, live in California and Virginia. Carole's grown sons work in Hollywood as successful movie makers. She has one grandchild, Mac Weaver, born in February 2016.

BONUS MATERIAL!

Go to www.caroleweaverlinsner.com to access your bonus video: "A Guided Tour Through the Art of Carole's Home!"

In this video you will join me on a short tour of some of the art in my home. Beyond the works we've visited here in *Side Effects*, you'll experience some other art treasures I love. Some speak to me of healing power, others of the artist's struggle, and some just make my endorphins flow! You'll find more of my daily art companions I want to share with you: Artifacts of joy and wisdom.

Go to www.caroleweaverlinsner.com and enter your name and e-mail and you will receive the link to this video tour and commentary.

CPSIA information can be obtained
at www.ICGtesting.com
Printed in the USA
JSHW030959250920
8206JS00006B/22